Fluid Space and Transformational Learning

T0299845

Fluid Space and Transformational Learning presents a critique of the interlocking questions of 'school architecture' and education and attempts to establish a field of questioning that aspectualises and intersects concepts, theories and practices connected with the contemporary school building and the deschooling of learning and of the space within and through which it takes place.

Tying together the historicity of architectural theory, criticism and practice and the plural dynamic of social fields and sciences, this book outlines the qualities and modalities of experiential fields of transformational learning.

The three qualities of space that are highlighted along the way – activated, polyphonic and playful space – as they emerge (without being instrumentalised) through architecturalised spatial modalities – flexibility, variability, interactivity, taut fluid polyphony, multiplicity, transcendence of boundaries – tend to construct and establish a school environment rich in heretical sociospatial codes.

Meshing cooperative, participatory, intrapsychic and interpsychic dimensions, they invite the factors of learning to a creative, imponderable, transformational disorder and deconstruct dominant conditioned reflexes of a disciplinary, methodical and productive order.

Kyriaki Tsoukala is Professor of Architectural Theory at the School of Architecture, Aristotle University of Thessaloniki. She has published six authored books, twelve edited books and many articles on the subjects of the perception of space, the new qualities of public space and the epistemological issues of contemporary architecture.

Routledge Focus on Design Pedagogy

The Routledge Focus on Design Pedagogy series provides the reader with the latest scholarship for instructors who educate designers. The series publishes research from across the globe and covers areas as diverse as beginning design and foundational design, architecture, product design, interior design, fashion design, landscape architecture, urban design, and architectural conservation and historic preservation. By making these studies available to the worldwide academic community, the series aims to promote quality design education.

Fluid Space and Transformational Learning
Kyriaki Tsoukala

Fluid Space and Transformational Learning

Kyriaki Tsoukala

**With a prologue by
Nikolaos-Ion Terzoglou**

LONDON AND NEW YORK

First published 2017 by Routledge

2 Park Square, Milton Park, Abingdon, Oxon, OX14 4RN
605 Third Avenue, New York, NY 10017

Routledge is an imprint of the Taylor & Francis Group, an informa business

First issued in paperback 2020

British Library Cataloguing-in-Publication Data
A catalogue record for this book is available from the British Library

Library of Congress Cataloging-in-Publication Data
A catalog record for this book has been requested

ISBN: 978-1-138-62893-9 (hbk)
ISBN: 978-0-367-73636-1 (pbk)

Typeset in Times New Roman
by Apex CoVantage, LLC

To Paraskevas,
for our years of fraternal dialogical drifting

Contents

List of figures   viii
Acknowledgements   x
Prologue   xi
NIKOLAOS-ION TERZOGLOU

Introduction   1

1 Stimulative learning   4

**2 The architecture of educational modality:
     qualities of space**   12
Quality 1: activated space 14
Quality 2: dialogical-polyphonic space 16
Quality 3: playful space 19

3 From qualities to modalities   22
Modality 1: flexibility, transformability, interactivity 22
Modality 2: liquidity, taut fluidity 32
*Modality 3: breadth of form, multiplicity, transcending
     boundaries 53*

**A few final words: fluid space and transformational
learning**   62

Bibliography   66
Index   69

Figures

3.1a   School complex in Suresnes (1935–36). Architects:
Lods & Beaudouin. Floor plans.   24

3.1b   School complex in Suresnes (1935–36). The classroom-
pavilion.   24

3.2a   Corona School in Los Angeles (1935). Architect:
R. Neutra. Classrooms.   25

3.2b   Impington Hall in Cambridgeshire (1936). Architects:
W. Gropius & M. Fry. Classrooms.   25

3.3   Aghios Dimitrios Gymnasium-Lyceum, Athens
(1969–1974). Design: Takis Zenetos. Ground plan
of a typical floor in the school's first and third
operating phase.   27

3.4   Paul Chevalier school complex in Rillieux-la-Pape,
Lyon (2013). Design: Tectoniques. View of part
of the building.   31

3.5a   Apollo schools in Amsterdam (1980). Design:
H. Hertzberger. View of the central common space.   35

3.5b   Apollo schools in Amsterdam. View of the central
common space.   36

3.6   Apollo schools in Amsterdam (1980). Design:
H. Hertzberger. Floor plans and section.   37

3.7   Montessori College Oost, Amsterdam (1999). Architect:
H. Hertzberger. Floor plans and section.   38

3.8   Montessori College Oost, Amsterdam (1999). Architect:
H. Hertzberger. View of the central common space.   39

3.9   St Benno School, Dresden (1996). Design: G. Behnisch.
Floor plans and east façade.   41

3.10a   St Benno School. Interior common space.   42

3.10b   St Benno School. Interior common space.   42

3.11a	Albert Schweitzer School in Bad Rappenau (1991). Architect: G. Behnisch. Ground floor plan and section.	43
3.11b	Albert Schweitzer School in Bad Rappenau (1991). Architect: G. Behnisch. Interior common space.	43
3.12a	Youth Music School, Hamburg (1997–2000). Design: E. Miralles & B. Tagliabue. Maquette.	45
3.12b	Youth Music School, Hamburg (1997–2000). Floor plans.	45
3.13	Youth Music School, Hamburg (1997–2000). Interior common space.	46
3.14a	Youth Music School, Hamburg (1997–2000). Interior common space.	47
3.14b	Youth Music School, Hamburg (1997–2000). View of the interior common space.	47
3.15	Manuel Belgrano School, Cordoba, Argentina (1960–1971). Design: O. Bidinost, J. Chute. Floor plans and section.	49
3.16a	Manuel Belgrano School, Cordoba, Argentina (1960–1971). Design: O. Bidinost, J. Chute. Views of the semi-cover space.	50
3.16b	Manuel Belgrano School, Cordoba, Argentina (1960–1971). Views of the semi-cover space.	51
3.17a	Manuel Belgrano School, Cordoba, Argentina (1960–1971). View of the building.	51
3.17b	Manuel Belgrano School, Cordoba, Argentina (1960–1971). View of the semi-cover space.	52
3.18a	Montessori School, Delft (1966–70). Brick podium block.	55
3.18b	Montessori School, Delft (1966–70). Brick podium block.	55
3.19a	METI School, Rudrapur, Bangladesh (2005–2006). Design: A. Heringer. View of the building.	58
3.19b	METI School, Rudrapur, Bangladesh (2005–2006). Floor plans and section.	59
3.20a	METI School, Rudrapur, Bangladesh (2005–2006). Interior learning space.	59
3.20b	METI School, Rudrapur, Bangladesh (2005–2006). Interior common space.	60

Acknowledgements

I wish to thank the external reviewers of the initial book proposal for their important comments and suggestions. Also, I would like to extend my sincere thanks to the editors Grace Harrison and Sadé Lee at Routledge/Taylor and Francis for their support of the project. Particular thanks are owed to the Hellenic Institute of Architecture; to the architectural firms of Behnisch & Partners, Herman Hertzberger, Anna Heringer and Tectoniques; to the periodical *El Croquis*; to photographers Kurt Hoerbst and Christian Kandzia; to architects Claudio Conenna and Ismael Eyras; and to Veronica Bidinost, for their gracious permission to use material for the illustrations appearing in this book.

Prologue

Nikolaos-Ion Terzoglou*

Conceptual dimensions of space in Kyriaki Tsoukala's theoretical production

The main objective of this prologue is to offer a succinct and concise presentation of certain basic epistemological questions, conceptual dimensions and philosophical problems that arise in relation to the question of space. The occasion for these thoughts is Kyriaki Tsoukala's recent book *Fluid Space and Transformational Learning*. Along with a brief commentary on the work, I shall endeavour to correlate certain of its key themes with the author's earlier theoretical production, especially her book *Trends in School Design: From Child-Centred Functionalism to the Post-Modern Approach* (hereinafter *Trends*) (Tsoukala 2000b). It is of course still too early to evaluate this continually intensified and expanded theoretical output as a whole. Professor Tsoukala's contribution to contemporary Greek and international theory and criticism of architecture is multiple and significant, and it constitutes an open-ended work in progress. Purely by way of example, let me mention that in just the past six years (2009–2015), she has written, edited or co-edited seven books, a by no means negligible achievement.

Tsoukala's intervention into the contemporary theoretical discussion on space sprang from the complex relation between architecture and psychology, with an emphasis on the child's relation to the architectural and urban environment (Tsoukala 2000a). This exploration gradually expanded from the school building to the neighbourhood and, finally, to the public space of the city (Tsoukala 2001, 2006). This broadening of her subject matter and perspective later (or simultaneously) sparked a cycle of analyses on the structure, organisation and meaning of public space in contemporary Western societies, stressing its transformations in the context of late capitalism and globalisation (Tsoukala 2008). This series of recent analyses operates on multiple methodological levels, intermeshing the psychological dimension of space with the sociological interpretation and political texture of the architectural and urban configurations of hyper-modernity.

A continual expansion of her conceptual toolkit has enabled her to penetrate the complexity of these social, political and economic developments: apart from the expected references to the history and theory of architecture, we find in her texts borrowings from the human sciences, psychoanalysis, semiology and semantics, political science, cultural theory, linguistics and philosophy. The point at which these currents and tools of thinking converge is space and its meaning. At the same time as she worked on the foregoing studies, her contact with the complex structure of architectural and urban space constantly prompts her in an endeavour to develop critical appreciations and evaluations of the works of major architects and examples of materialisation of emblematic spatial configurations, whether these belong to the past – remote or recent – or contemporary times. Particularly valuable works in this field are the collective studies on Louis Kahn (Conenna, Pantelidou & Tsoukala 2013) and Enric Miralles (Conenna, Tsoukala et al. 2014).

Psychology of perceptual space, sociology and political analysis of public space and also critique of architectural praxis are the three intersecting poles, the three thematic nuclei, the *three plateaus of thought* of the multifaceted theoretical output of a writer and teacher who displays a remarkable ability to assimilate and co-ordinate heterogeneous fields and pieces of information into substantially cohesive sets and subsets of concepts. In my inevitable simplification these three levels of thinking are not easily harmonised, nor do they suggest an obvious dialectic. Each one has its own peculiar methods of analysis and interpretive perspective of 'things', of its corresponding empirical material. Tsoukala seems to handle this diversity pluralistically, without necessarily wanting to reduce it to the austerity of a unified method. How might this multiplicity and openness be explained? Let us begin with some words of her own, an aphorism that provides promising ground for a possible answer to this question. For Tsoukala, architecture is 'a field of dramatisation of concepts and ideas, . . . an area for the development of social practices' (Tsoukala 2009: 6). In her first study, *Trends*, she writes that 'architecture is not only a product of aesthetics or technology, but in its form and content imprints value systems and behaviour models characteristic of its social context' (Tsoukala 2000b: 165).

If, beyond current, conventional, empirical notions, we accept that space and architecture cannot be reduced simply to the solution of a technical problem or an aesthetic formula but have a deeper interaction with the social and cultural field, then the question automatically arises as to the social dimension of space, the social structure of place and the cultural meaning of architecture. Each space is 'produced' by a specific community and is imbued with living practices and meanings of life that correspond to a given stage of historical, economic and philosophical development. The 'production of space' (Lefebvre 2000) brings together material structures and imaginary meanings in a defined, differentiated whole. Architecture is an organic part of this total cultural process. It is not identified with simply 'building' or the construction of edifices. Going beyond the formalistic and technological interpretations of architecture, refusing any such reduction, Tsoukala opens the architectural discipline to the human sciences, to the risk of a conceptual broadening of the architectural phenomenon so as to include political and moral problems, moving – in her own words – in the 'uncertain paths of interdisciplinarity' (Tsoukala 2012: 63).

If architecture is a 'dramatisation of concepts', the primary field of this dramatisation is space. Architectural spaces are the realisation of philosophical ideas. The idea of 'space', with its multiple adventures and transformations in the twentieth century (Terzoglou 2009), permits Tsoukala to orchestrate a network of interdisciplinary intersections of architecture with the domains of society and culture. With these intersections come questions about the boundaries, the rules, the methodological presuppositions and the nature of architecture as a discipline, in its interaction with the sciences of human culture. An exceptionally difficult equilibrium opens up between the analysis and the synthesis of space, the empirical and the normative, what exists and what should exist and also facts and values. Inevitable complications of architectural thinking emerge when the risk of interdisciplinarity is undertaken. It is, then, Tsoukala's initial epistemological position and avowal, her refusal to restrict architecture to the narrow framework of an academic formalism that explains the diversity of her theoretical production and guides her choice of conceptual and methodological tools.

In *Trends*, the study that formed the prehistory of the book I analyse here, these multiple tools are applied to explore the relationships among the school environment, the educational theories and practices accommodated there, and the child's perception and appropriation of the space. The historical horizon for the interaction of school buildings as a material production of space with the subjective experience of the children inhabiting it spans most of the twentieth century, with a brief mention of the latter part of the nineteenth century. Tsoukala schematises this interaction into *four phases or stages*: child-centred functionalism, industrial mass production, the scientification of design and the social approach of post-modernism (Tsoukala 2000b: 12–13). The complexity of the epistemological issues raised by Tsoukala's interdisciplinarity is evident in this early study. In it, she does not confine herself to an analysis of school building types and their 'Euclidian geometry' but instead attempts to reveal its interweaving with 'social geometry' (Tsoukala 2000b: 11). That is with the modes of distribution of pupils, teachers and their physical bodies within the space of the school based on the pedagogical perceptions of each era, Tsoukala makes continual use of conceptual tools that refer to different dimensions of space. The generality and inherent ambiguity of the concept of 'space' allow her to speak at the same time of its material structure, of its social organisation – 'social space' (2000b: 50) – and of its psychological quality. The hidden epistemological acceptance behind this choice seems to me to be *the isomorphism of spatial organisation and social structure*. On one hand, teacher-centred education 'corresponds' to a closed spatial model that is monological and homogeneous: the 'classroom'. On the other, the 'new education', which emphasises children's independent self-activity and initiative, group work and the unity of theory and practice, generates a space that is flexible, complex, convertible and fluid, which gradually eliminates the whole concept of the classroom and ushers in classroom-free schooling.

Tsoukala interlaces into her account appropriate theoretical analyses (e.g. of the concept of child-scale) and empirical descriptions of realised architectural examples that demonstrate the aforementioned isomorphism. These confirm the working hypothesis that sustains interdisciplinarity as a methodological choice: space really has a historical-cultural value and bears the traces of social processes and psychological qualities. Here, however, a difficult question arises, a problem indissolubly linked with that method: what 'space', precisely, are we talking about? 'Fluid space' (Tsoukala 2000b: 51, 61, 115), 'activated space' (2000b: 109), 'intermediate-transitional space' (102), 'space of play' (41), 'flexible, convertible space' (76) are all thoroughly analysed in the book, but *to what conceptual level of space* do they refer – to its material constitution, its social organisation, its (potential) educational use or its psychological appropriation/perception? There is no easy answer, because the 'qualities of space' that Tsoukala analyses (163) seem to endlessly hang in mid-air among all these levels.

The same or similar questions are raised by the sequel to that study, the book we have here: *Fluid Space and Transformational Learning*. It extends the consideration of the relations between school environment, social structures, educational theories and the psychology of child perception to the two decades that just passed (1990–2010), covering the time gap left by the previous work. Here, she emphasises the evolutions that marked the school environment during the period of globalisation, late capitalism and hyper-modernity – that is when the fluidity of social space is reflected in the trend towards deschooling the educational process into differentiated and constantly changing learning landscapes. The difference in relation to the previous work lies in the renewed conceptual armoury that the author uses. In the fourteen years since *Trends*, Tsoukala has opened up the *two new plateaus of thought* that refer to contemporary public space and the analysis of emblematic modernist and postmodernist works of architecture, and 'applied' this rich experience to a new and deeper penetration of the school environment, enriching it with patterns of thinking drawn from cultural theory, cultural criticism, philosophy and politics. The conceptual categories of space are thus presented with greater breadth, depth and complexity. Instead of a temporal classification into four thematic/epistemic trends in design, Tsoukala here chooses to organise the built, empirical material (of school buildings) on the basis of three strategic spatial concepts or spatial qualities: 'activated', 'dialogical/polyphonic' and 'playful'. It is true that at least one of these concepts ('activated space') had already been developed and constituted at the time *Trends* was published, but here it is reworked in the light of finds from the other plateaus of thought, and at the same time, it is enriched with political resonances produced in its dialectical relation with the other two.

The book is dense. It generates a new cycle of epistemological questions even more pressing than the first. These are related to the author's core choice of defining a logical sequence in the structure of the book and the argument that heads from an educational contemplation to 'modalities of space', via the three qualities or characters of space mentioned earlier. The first question that arises is whether this sequence is binding, deterministically stated and causal. In other words, does the 'stimulative learning' that condenses contemporary relational-centred education, with its emphasis on *affective-emotional experience*, lead inescapably to the 'production' of these specific spatial qualities? And do these spatial qualities necessarily lead to the three corresponding modalities? Would it be possible for new modalities of space to create spatial qualities that would in turn fire transformations in education theory? In other words, is school space in hyper-modernity the visible imprint, the trace of the dominant educational conception; or is it possible for architectural design to supply changes in the structure of educational thinking? This question is linked to the initial hypothesis of the isomorphism of social structure and spatial organisation. If this isomorphism is valid, then why could we not be led from the modality of space to a theory of education rather than the other way about?

The second question that arises from this triple dialectic asks how 'qualities' differ from 'modalities'. Put another way, *at what level* does the quality of space constitute itself as a concept? If we accept that modalities express versions of shaping – ways of materialising, declaring and demonstrating – spatial qualities in real, built architectural space, this would mean that 'qualities' are more abstract as entities and do not necessarily have a specific material articulation or implementation. What 'space', then, are we talking about when we describe a 'quality of space'? Let us take an example: 'activated space'. In *Trends*, Tsoukala defined activated space as 'the environment that does not respond mechanically to the action of the child upon it but is engaged as a socio-cultural object in the motives and aims of the child's activities' (Tsoukala 2000b: 109). In *Fluid Space and Transformational Learning*, we learn that this space is also flexible and variable, permitting its socio-practical correlation with the child in a collaborative educational framework. It is now clear that 'space' here refers to an intermediate, dangling stage or level, which also has both social qualities – which borrow lineaments from the conceptual environment of the culture and from the pedagogical context – and certain faint, vague, indefinite, quasi-geometrical – albeit imprecisely determined – qualities. The modalities that 'correspond' to it are flexibility, variability and interactivity. Since, however, these are analysed here through specific examples of built architecture, these modalities seem in fact to concentrate and refer to empirical cases of materialisation of spatial qualities or characters in the 'real world'.

I would like to propose as a working hypothesis that the qualities of space, the three focal concepts that Tsoukala uses in *Fluid Space and Transformational Learning*, resemble methodologically what Max Weber called an 'ideal type'. According to Weber,

> The ideal typical concept will help to develop our skill in imputation in *research*: it is no 'hypothesis', but it offers guidance to the construction of hypotheses . . . An ideal type is formed by the one-sided *accentuation* of one or more points of view and by the synthesis of a great many diffuse, discrete, more or less present and occasionally absent concrete individual phenomena, which are arranged according to those one-sidedly emphasized viewpoints into a unified analytical construct (Gedankenbild). In its conceptual purity, this mental construct cannot be found empirically anywhere in reality. It is a utopia. Historical research faces the task of determining in each individual case, the extent to which this ideal-construct approximates to or diverges from reality.
>
> (Weber 1949: 90)

Tsoukala appears to work on the basis of 'ideal types': 'activated' space, 'dialogical/polyphonic' space and 'playful' space are conceptual abstractions, mental images that allow disparate social properties, multiple morphological features and differentiated spatial structures to be grouped into an explanatory scheme. This scheme is then used as a rule – as a normative ideal for evaluation and analysis, interpretation and classification – of the empirical material of the built school architecture. I would go so far as to say, moreover, that they encapsulate demands and postulations from the author that are posited as axiomatic, a priori structures of the mind. This abstract order of discourse, with its inherent ambiguity, allows Tsoukala to bridge the distances created by the risk of interdisciplinarity: from

Lewin's field theory, Vygotsky's zone of proximal development, Bakhtin's differential dialogicality and Lacan's void to the built educational spaces of Miralles, Behnisch, Bidinost and Hertzberger, the ideotypical 'qualities of space' link the abstract with the concrete, the normative with the descriptive and concept with matter. Quite apart, then, from its several particular contributions to contemporary theory and design of school space, *Fluid Space and Transformational Learning* has, in my view, a decidedly methodological value, demonstrating a possible way of moving from abstract ideas to specific material results. Tsoukala shows how activated space favours the collaboration and 'responsiveness' of the built structure's materiality, how dialogical space permits meetings and co-existence in an open-ended place of the potential, a perpetual, intensive, multiple and fluid reconciliation of the individual with the environment, and how playful space fosters the de-symbolisation of established meanings, throwing open a field of freedom, fissures and events, imponderable experience and rambling. These descriptions will lead me to certain final questions and conclusions.

Is there a historicity of these ideal types of space? Which are the layers of theoretical elaborations that would possibly allow us to speak of their genealogy? Let us take 'playful space' first. This space expresses an important dimension of urban public space, the fragmentary and random patchwork of 'situations' that lies at the root of the heterogeneous space of direct participation: the collage of multicultural activities accommodated by every genuine public space (Tsoukala 2012: 66) opens up difference as a precondition of democracy. Play can thus be conducive to a meeting with otherness (2012: 69). The genealogy of this ideal type could be sought in the situationists and the importance they ascribed to the role of play for the transformation of the city they envisaged (Sadler 1998: 34–35, 77, 120). 'Dialogical space' can plainly be traced back to Bakhtin's thinking on utterance as speech interaction, in combination with Vygotsky's theory of the importance of intersubjective *activity* in the constitution of an energetic, communicative, participative subject. This subject is created socially. 'Dialogical space', which is the expression and the core of this type of subject, is the quality that enables it to acquire meaning through the performative social practices that it accommodates (Tsoukala 2010b: 407–411). As Tsoukala says, 'If architectural space is not to degrade to the level of utility and fetishisation, or contribute to the alienation of the subject through a spatial pseudo-activity, it must seek performative forms of spatial activity, dialogical, not monological' (Tsoukala 2010b: 416).

'Activated space' seems to have a more complex origin. I can see an affinity between this ideal type and similar concepts from gestalt psychology and

phenomenology. We are familiar with the frequent influence of phenomenology on post-war psychological thinking, as demonstrated by Moles and
Rohmer (1972: 7–62, 157–158) or, conversely, its psychological roots (Husserl 1997: xxv, 42; Moran & Mooney 2002: 59–61). 'Activated space' brings
to mind Koffka's 'behavioural space', a lived space of symbolic qualities
and meanings (Tsoukala 2006: 50, 2007: 52). It is even more reminiscent of
Lewin's life-space (*espace vital*). The life-space predicated by Lewin, who
was a collaborator of Köhler and proponent of a topological field psychology, resembles Tsoukala's 'activated space' to the degree that both express
a dialectical conception of the equivalent interaction of subject and environment in the creation of the lived representation of space (Tsoukala 2001:
23, 2006: 50–51, 2007: 52–53). Both views may perhaps be traced back
to a common philosophical root: the concept of *Lebenswelt* ('life-world')
as developed by Edmund Husserl in *The Crisis of European Sciences and
Transcendental Phenomenology*. The everyday surrounding life-world, says
Husserl, is a world of immediate, personal, lived experience of space which
is invested with forms of meaning (Husserl 2002: 152–157, 163–165). The
participation of the individual in this living environment of meaning is
mediated by the organic living body (*Leib*), which Husserl distinguishes
from the physical body (*Körper*) (Husserl 2002: 153–154). The living body
constructs, through actions and intuitions, a common, *intersubjective world
of meaning*, an environment (*Umgebung*) – to recall his 1907 lectures entitled *Thing and Space* (Husserl 1997: 1–4).

This brings to the fore the ideological, notional dimension of activated
life-space, which coexists with its lived, bodily texture: life-space has
acquired symbolic traits and has drawn meaning from an activated consciousness. Indeed, the studies co-authored by Tsoukala and Germanos
stress the importance of the dimension of 'notional and mental space' for
perceptual psychology and seek its 'range' and 'form', using mental map-
ping as their primary tool (Tsoukala & Germanos 2000: 86, 99). This conceptual dimension of activated space might perhaps stem from the dominant
idea of the neo-Kantian Jean Piaget, who saw knowledge as an active construction of reality – an idea which, in direct opposition to behaviourism
and the passive reception of stimuli from the environment, presupposes an
'active organism', a vital involvement in the construction of the meaning
of space (Piaget & Inhelder 1967: 447–449, 454; Tsoukala 2001: 41, 2006:
40–42, 49–50, 2007: 40–43, 51–52). I have dealt in a more detailed way
with the architectural consequences of the ideotype of 'activated space' in
an earlier study (Terzoglou 2012: 88–90). In connection with the concept
of 'activated space', and as a sort of conclusion, I would like to formu-
late a more general working hypothesis about the conceptual dimensions of
space in the thinking of Kyriaki Tsoukala. We have seen how the openness
of her theoretical production permits different levels of the constitution of

spatiality, from the abstract to the most specific, to converse and correlate with one another. The question is, is there a hierarchy among them? Is there a privileged level that underlies all the rest? I think there is. And I presume that it is linked to the solid phenomenological root of her thinking. This root is evident in phrases as such these: 'Lived space transcends geometric space' (Tsoukala 2000a: 12); 'the human/living organism and his bodily space, which expresses the spatiality of his existence, sensible and intellectual' (9); 'the inscription of existential space on material, real space will overturn the formalistic and naturalistic perception of space' (12). Tsoukala's privileged ideotype is 'bodily space', the space of meaningful actions and everyday practices. Savvas Kontaratos (1983) has systematised this tradition of thought with great perspicuity. And Tsoukala herself has identified the primary role of the body in the postmodern and hyper-modern condition of architectural practice: 'The meaningless void acquires meaning in moving from the concept (modernity) to the body (post-hyper-modernity)' (Tsoukala 2010a: 29).

This notwithstanding, let us not hastily assign Tsoukala to a contemporary version of phenomenology. Her complex thinking cannot easily be reduced to that character alone. While she shares many themes with phenomenology (lived experience versus geometry and role of the body in the formation of spatial experience), I think that there is a crucial and telling difference between them: in Tsoukala's work, the 'body' is not just the individual, personal body of each discrete subject; it also refers to the *plural body of the social whole*. Her central question seems to be how architecture can permit the transition from the individual body to the social body, how it can articulate the preconditions for the construction of the social body. She emphasises that insistence on descriptive performance and direct, unmediated bodily action does not necessarily lead to the constitution of the social (Tsoukala 2012: 73). Establishing 'a poetics of the space of coordinated and transformative bodily experience' requires a deeper change. Unlike John Peponis's *Spatial Choreographies*, Tsoukala's fluid spaces are not inscribed simply in a descriptive morphology of the perceptual, sensory experience of the visual architectural culture (Peponis 1997: 14). They demand a participative transposition in the institutional, economic and authoritative mechanisms that organise that culture (Tsoukala 2010b: 413). In the thinking of Kyriaki Tsoukala, in other words, the conceptual dimensions of space meet a request that is material, social and *political*.

September 2015

Note

* Nikolaos-Ion Terzoglou is an Assistant Professor on Architectural Concepts and Theories at the National Technical University of Athens, Greece.

xx *Prologue*

Bibliography

Conenna, Claudio, Pantelidou, Lila & Tsoukala, Kyriaki (eds.) (2013). *The Teaching of Louis I. Kahn and Other Essays*. Thessaloniki: Epikentro Editions (In Greek).

Conenna, Claudio, Tsoukala, Kyriaki et al. (eds.) (2014). *Enric Miralles, Architect*. Thessaloniki: Epikentro Editions (In Greek).

Husserl, Edmund (1997). *Thing and Space: Lectures of 1907*. Translated by Richard Rojcewicz. Dordrecht, Boston and London: Kluwer Academic.

Husserl, Edmund (2002). "The Way into Phenomenological Transcendental Philosophy by Inquiring Back From the Pregiven Life-World." In: *The Phenomenology Reader*, edited by Dermot Moran & Timothy Mooney, 151–174. London and New York: Routledge.

Kontaratos, Savvas (1983). *The Experience of Architectural Space and the Body Image*. Athens: Kastanioti Editions (In Greek).

Lefebvre, Henri (2000). *La Production de l'Espace*. Paris: Anthropos.

Moles, A. Abraham & Rohmer, Élisabeth (1972). *Psychologie de l'Espace*. Tournai: Casterman.

Moran, Dermot & Mooney, Timothy (eds.) (2002). *The Phenomenology Reader*. London and New York: Routledge.

Peponis, John (1997). *Spatial Choreographies: The Architectural Shaping of Meaning*. Athens: Alexandreia Editions (In Greek).

Piaget, Jean & Inhelder, Bärbel (1967). *The Child's Conception of Space*. Translated by Frances J. Langdon & Justus L. Lunzer. New York: W.W. Norton.

Sadler, Simon (1998). *The Situationist City*. Cambridge, MA and London: The MIT Press.

Terzoglou, Nikolaos-Ion (2009). *Ideas of Space in the Twentieth Century*. Athens: Nissos Editions (In Greek).

Terzoglou, Nikolaos-Ion (2012). "'Activated' Public Spaces in the Contemporary City: Philosophical and Architectural Approaches." In: *youth.www.public space: Undisciplined Gatherings + Oblique Passages*, edited by Kyriaki Tsoukala, Charikleia Pantelidou et al., 77–91. Thessaloniki: Epikentro Editions (In Greek).

Tsoukala, Kyriaki (2000a). "Introduction." In: *Architecture, Child and Education*, edited by Kyriaki Tsoukala, 7–14. Thessaloniki: Paratiritis Editions (In Greek).

Tsoukala, Kyriaki (2000b). *Trends in School Design: From Child-Centred Functionalism to the Post-Modern Approach*. 2nd edition, supplemented, revised. Thessaloniki: Paratiritis Editions (In Greek).

Tsoukala, Kyriaki (2001). *L'Image de la Ville chez l'Enfant*. Paris: Anthropos/Economica.

Tsoukala, Kyriaki (2006). *Children's Urban Locality: Architecture and Mental Representations of Space*. Athens: Typothito Editions (In Greek).

Tsoukala, Kyriaki (2007). *Les Territoires Urbains de l'Enfant*. Paris: L'Harmattan.

Tsoukala, Kyriaki (2008). "Public Space: Limits and Identity in the Era of Globalisation." In: *Inter-culturalism, Globalisation and Identities*, edited by Eleni Hontolidou, Grigoris Pashalides, Kyriaki Tsoukala & Andreas Lazaris, 149–157. Athens: Gutenberg (In Greek).

Tsoukala, Kyriaki (2009). "Editorial". *ELSA, Environment, Land, Society: Architectonics* 1 (3–4): 6.

Tsoukala, Kyriaki (2010a). "Introduction: Postmodern Viewpoints." In: *Postmodern Viewpoints*, edited by Kyraki Tsoukala, Maria N. Daniil & Charikleia Pantelidou, 15–50. Thessaloniki: Epikentro Editions (In Greek).

Tsoukala, Kyriaki (2010b). "Lacan and Vygotsky: 'Void' and 'Dialogical' Space." In: *Postmodern Viewpoints*, edited by Kyriaki Tsoukala, Maria N. Daniil & Charikleia Pantelidou, 393–423. Thessaloniki: Epikentro Editions (In Greek).

Tsoukala, Kyriaki (2012). "Inter-humanity and Corporeality in the 'Youthful' Diversions of Public Space." In: *youth.www.public space: Undisciplined Gatherings + Oblique Passages*, edited by Kyriaki Tsoukala, Charikleia Pantelidou et al., 63–75. Thessaloniki: Epikentro Editions (In Greek).

Tsoukala, Kyriaki & Germanos, Dimitris (2000). "From the Perception and Valuation of Space to Design: Interventions in Thermi's Outdoor Spaces Aiming at the Creation of an Appropriate Environment for Teenagers." In: *Architecture, Child and Education*, edited by Kyriaki Tsoukala, 71–114. Thessaloniki: Paratiritis Editions (In Greek).

Weber, Max (1949). "'Objectivity' in Social Science and Social Policy." In: *The Methodology of the Social Sciences*, edited by Edward A. Shils & Henry A. Finch, 49–112. Glencoe, IL: The Free Press.

Introduction

This work will pursue and enrich the subject matter with which we have dealt in the past concerning school architecture in the twentieth century. That book is suffused with the logic of an unfolding within social-historical-cultural time of the perceptions governing the organisation of teaching spaces in the Western world, and especially in Europe. It encounters trends and spatial categories stemming from other fields, such as the history of architecture, and highlights particularities proximate to the domain of school architecture that are due to its vital ties with teaching and educational policy in general. The study does not cover the whole century, but concludes with the decades of the 1970s and 1980s – that is the first phase of post-modernism in architecture. It refers synoptically to this phenomenon, describing the marks it has left on school architecture through examples of structuralism and the trends of historicism, metaphor and meaning.

Here, we shall examine in more detail the post-postmodern period, known as the age of hyper-modernity, or globalisation, essentially the last two decades, thus chronologically completing the previous work but approaching it in a different way. Our object is not to register and interpret the different trends, but to ask questions, to critique, to unfold concepts and theories relating to contemporary school buildings and the deschooling of learning and the space within which it takes place. Examples of contemporary learning environments and others from earlier periods that can be considered heralds of today's thinking and its applications in the Western world are presented with critical commentary.

We will begin by outlining the interrelations between the two fields, 'school' architecture and teaching/education, and how they mesh with other fields of knowledge, in an attempt to identify common concepts that shape the strands of pedagogic thinking and, naturally, the lines of the architectural process in the 'fields of learning'. At the same time we shall be moving in experimental fields with which we have engaged in the past in the framework of specific epistemological considerations, and in that context proposing concepts that project into current thinking and which in later studies we have attempted to correlate with key concepts of other cognitive fields, revealing the common ground in a fluid, differentiated and continuously variable conceptual landscape. As with the question of 'school' architecture, so with that of teaching, of the theories and practices of learning, our focus is not on registering and interpreting contemporary trends – how indeed could we attempt such a thing in the case of pedagogy? – but on confining ourselves to demonstrating a trend in ways of learning in a time of electronic and globalised culture.

The first chapter of our study deals with a cohesive consideration of active-cooperative-communicative/dialogical-experiential learning in our modern societies, within a temporal framework guided less by chronological and historical than by conceptual and epistemological criteria (immersed nonetheless in their historicity). Our approach is based not on the linear logic of a retrospective quest for the origin and evolution of the concepts but on that of distinguishing their fine shades of difference, their congruent and divergent aspects, which helps constitute a critical discourse, shape views about what is happening in teaching practice, and consequently construct a conceptual corpus for an architecture of dialogically and corporeally coordinated spatial-temporal experience. In this first chapter we will touch on, as an underpinning for the nexus of dialogical-experiential teaching practice, Vygotsky's concepts of activity, the signs of cultural systems, psychological tools and the zone of proximal development (interactivity, collaboration). Here we shall meet their relation with Bakhtinian concepts of dialogicality, polyphony and heteroglossia and with Lacanian concepts of passive activity, absence/void, the Other, otherness. These theories seem to form the substratum of contemporary trends in education and to be reflected in the complex contemporary field of a pedagogy that seeks to keep its distance from an active but largely guided learning process.

In the second chapter we attempt to give form and substance to spatial qualities that stem from the foregoing approach and forge the image of an 'other', different, space for learning, permuting the very term that until recently rendered this function. The school or educational building associated with the concept of the classroom is renamed a learning field or – if we adopt Hertzberger's term – a learning landscape. The dividing lines between school and society, teacher and taught, different ages and roles, become boundaries constantly shifting within a climate of freedom and interactivity, collaboration and cooperation, traversing and broadening the dynamic process of learning and its factors. We will comment on the course of the concept of open space and how it has changed over time. In a previous work, *Trends in School Architecture: From Child-Centred Functionality to the Post-Modern Approach*, we dealt extensively with open-plan and other forms of open school environments linked with the open teaching movement of the first half of the twentieth century and the two decades that shouldered the burden of rebuilding societies in the wake of the devastation wreaked by the Second World War. References to certain elements of that first study on questions of school space will be handled from a different point of view and re-assessed in the contemporary conditions in which educational processes are shaped and instituted. This perspective is woven (articulated) from three qualities/characteristics of space that at the same time constitute the criteria for the selection of examples for the 'learning landscapes'. These are: activated space, dialogical-polyphonic space and playful space. Putting these qualities in place is connected with, but not limited to, certain spatial properties, such as flexibility-variability-interactivity, fluid spatiality-taut fluidity and breadth of form-multiplicity-transcending boundaries, concepts that are developed in the third chapter.

Our study does not examine those propositions that are exclusively concerned with the form of the school building, disregarding the interior space where the educational activity takes place. We had similar examples from the period of the modern movement, excellent specimens of modern school architecture that did not, however, include the containing space in their otherwise revolutionary solutions, leaving untouched the traditional organisation of the classrooms and in general of school life. We see the same thing today in very attractive ideas for the innovative interaction between building and ground or shell and environment. We think, however, that these architectural examples are disconnected from contemporary innovative thinking on education and learning and consequently deficient as regards their capacity to satisfy today's covenant on everyday school life. That is why they have no place in a study that seeks to address the issue of the learning environment in its complexity – social, educational, psychological, cultural – without theoretical abstractions and simplifications that in the end create contradictory and partial solutions to contemporary habitational problems.

1   Stimulative learning

Like all other built environments, schools are places whose lines, organisation and spatial form bear values and meanings forged by the cultural making of our societies. The architecture of educational spaces correlates directly with the institutional framework of the educational system, and by extension with the attendant educational theory and practice. In order, therefore, to understand the architectural idiom that refers to these specific places, we shall turn to the science of education, drawing from that field the concepts that engage, communicate and interact with architecture. In this study our interest focuses on contemporary pedagogy, with its necessary links and references to older currents of educational thought and practice.

Contemporary pedagogy preserves principles of the new education, and at the same time incorporates concepts drawn from other fields, such as communication theory, systems theory, the theories of involvement and emotional experience. The difference between the new education and traditional pedagogy lies in the shift in focus to the dyadic relation between teacher and pupil. The perception behind the teaching and education offered in the institutional framework of the school system is no longer teacher-centred but child-centred. With the developments in the domain of psychology at the beginning of the twentieth century, and especially with the theories of Piaget, Binet and Bruner, pedagogy evolved into a science of psychopedagogy, absorbing (and transforming) the findings of developmental psychology. The child/pupil is recognised as an active member of the school community – not a passive one – (a Herbartian view later adopted by Alain), an enterprising individual with particular needs (different from those of adults and differentiated from those of his contemporaries). The interest shifts to the child, but remains on the dyadic relation between child and teacher (Ulmann 1982; Fragos 1983). This can be considered as the first radical change in the science of education. The shift in focus to the communication or relation that the child develops with the environment marks the second great moment in the science of education. If the constituents of education theory in the first half of the twentieth century are concentrated in the concept of 'child-centredness', what characterises contemporary pedagogy is the concept of communication, even though this is not new, having appeared in the work of Vygotsky (1934/1993, 1997) and Lewin (1959). It is not by accident that the two theorists were acquainted, worked together and met in Moscow, or that Lewin monitored the experimental research work of some of Vygotsky's associates in Berlin (Bakirtzis 2004). The *field theory* that Lewin introduced concerns the dynamic of human relations, the interactions and correlations between the members of social groups, the role of communication in the processes of construction of the self. Within the climate of his time, which was marked by extreme cultural and political phenomena, he turned his interest to communication between social groups, to the processes that generate changes and shifts in people's perceptions and attitudes, and to the mechanisms of resistance to change. His *field theory* dialectically links the individual with the collective, the psychological with the social, the intrapsychic with the interpsychic. The terms 'non-guidance' or 'absence' of the animator/teacher (whose involvement on the level of both form of communication and content is restricted to the minimum) are linked to the research activity of Lewin and his associates. He studied this dynamic co-existence and its effects on the development and constitution of the individual and blazed new research trails in the socio-psychological sciences.

In Vygotsky's theory the role of communication in the constitution of the individual is designated by the term 'zone of proximal development' and the terms 'external/internal speech' and 'psychological tool'. In his book *Thought and Language* (1934/1993) he points out that language is not only a means of representing human experience but also the *mental tool* that is used to construct, organise and re-construct thought. The emphasis is on the concept of *tool*, something we use to intervene in and modify nature. Studying human evolution, Vygotsky ascribes the beginning of thought to the twofold tool: the *technical* means of intervention in nature and the *symbol* which intervenes in functions of the mind. These two levels and kinds of functions of the tool cannot be separated. On the contrary, he stresses the single two-way dynamic coupling of transformations of man's internal and external nature through and within these tools, and argues against dualism and polarising schemas and against linear dialectics.

Language is considered as an intensely powerful symbolic system which is vigorous throughout life, and especially so in the early stages of a person's development. Thinking matures through speech, a process which follows the contradictory function that characterises the nature of things in general. That is language releases the child from many of the limitations imposed by his immediate object environment, but at the same time binds him to the system of models and meanings that he 'speaks'. The use of speech signs from infancy and early childhood creates a robust field of 'controlled potential' of the higher psychological processes on the level of *internalised speech*. Speech mediates the construction of perception, the intervention of memory, and other aspects of an individual's behaviour. The category of tools of the mind is held to include all products of culture (among them the built space, which marks its own rules of grammar and syntax).

The experiments carried out by Vygotsky and his associates substantiate the arguments he develops in his substantial – despite his short life – body of work. Technical tools-and-symbols involve the social environment in the construction of the higher mental functions. In his study *Mind in Society: The Development of Higher Psychological Processes* he writes that

> Every function in the child's cultural development appears twice: first, on the social level, and later, on the individual level; first, between people (*interpsychological*), and then inside the child (*intrapsychological*). This applies equally to voluntary attention, to logical memory, and to the formation of concepts. All the higher functions originate as actual relationships between individuals.
>
> (Vygotsky 1934/1997: 104)

For Vygotsky, language is a cultural tool that constructs and is constructed in the subject in the process of a dynamic dialectical condition which is also the generative vehicle of forms and transformations.

The concept of the 'psychological tool' is solidly linked with that of the 'activity' that ruptures the subject's relation of reproductive automatism with the symbolic condition and detaches him from his alienating relation with the Word. Vygotsky argues through a Marxist point of view that the motives and objectives of external activity set by society regulate the relation of the subject with the other and with his environment. When these motives and objectives ignore the subject's mental, social and emotional needs and do not involve him in the whole process of the activity by stimulating him with critical questions, then they turn it into a pseudo-activity – a pseudo-activity to the degree that its object and objective and the means for achieving it remain, for the subject, 'alien', incongruous and unfamiliar. They are shaped by others, and the subject is used as an engine for the reconstitution of a sterile symbolic order. The motives and objectives of the activities are not social and participatory, but private and operational.

Pseudo-activity results in alienation. Wittgenstein's term 'use', which replaced the term 'pseudo-activity' (Newman & Holzman 1996), could be used in this context. The use of language is not the same as language activity. Through simple use language is neutralised and leads to a fetishism, an arid symbolisation that thwarts the very nature of language as a cultural communicational tool that is transformed depending on the conditions in which it functions and takes shape. The use of language makes it a tool alienated from the person, whom it empowers through its symbolisation, reinforcing the symbolic order as shaped at other times and in other conditions which do not correspond to the needs of the individual. This is where the role of the form of the social construct enters, the characteristics that underlie its operation and are a function of the nature of the activity: activity or pseudo-activity/use.

One corollary of such a perception of the nature of activity is Vygotsky's concept of the zone of proximal development (ZPD). The ZPD is defined as activity-in-collaboration-with-others and differs from activity with others and individualised solitary activity. This concept – ZPD – denotes the intersubjective process of an activity during which the child is not required to learn something outside himself, external as regards his existence, but on the contrary makes him not a passive but a dialogical subject who contributes to the approach to knowledge (of the landscape of self-other-and-objects within societal limitary meanings). This complexity, reposing on the participatory, active and communicational form of the activity, constitutes the core of Vygotsky's thinking and his insistence on the role of learning in the shaping of awareness and radical practice. Indeed, ZPD itself is considered a revolutionary educational practice when it conduces, with other practices, to the non-alienated subject.

Working at the same time as Vygotsky, in the same place but in a different environment, was Bakhtin (Emerson 1983; Pesic & Baucal 1996). Freudian theory aroused opposition in the scientific and academic environment of the young, newly created socialist society. The work of Marx in this early period was an open theoretical system that admitted new facts and redefined itself within the new conditions so as to return to and reshape them. But in accordance with the new world view, which refused determinism and dualism, the relation of the individual with his environment is perceived as a single, open process. The perception of individual and environment is out, replaced by that of the individual-within-the-environment. There is no longer an interaction between two separate elements, but a single 'interactive/dialectical interchange' of elements within the same single situation.

Bakhtin attacks the dualism – as he understands it – of the conscious and the unconscious posited by Freud. He argues that conscious-and-unconscious both function and are shaped within the social context. By contrast, the reduction of the unconscious to the Id, to the individual's instincts and impulses, is what declassifies him socially (isolating him in family triangles). Elements of Bakhtin's critique of Freudian theory can be identified in Lacan, who seats division and conflict in the Word and not in impulses, with the difference that here, in Lacan's working proposition, the Word is oppressive as coming from the Other. It is what creates the gulf, the void, the absence, the abstraction of enjoyment. It is what imprisons the subject systemically in alienation. Bakhtin seats the Word in a dialogical environment and charges it with counteracting difference. The dialogical relation is a social-psychological concept proposed by the Marxist anti-psychology (anti-psychology in the sense of the rejection of the psychology that examines the individual as a phenomenon cut off from his social environment). The object of Bakhtin's 'hyperlinguistics' is not formulation but utterance – that is lectical interaction. Language is not reduced to a code (cf. structural linguistics and formalistic poetry), but is seen as a bridge linking persons. By emphasising dialogical lectical activity, Vygotsky and Bakhtin inscribe the Word/communication in historical-social space-time with its characteristic potential dynamic. Human morality is rooted in this sociability: in the recognition of the component element of the inter-human (Todorov 1994).

In recent decades, very interesting views have been expressed by teachers working in this direction within the new framework of environmental education (EE) and education for sustainable development (ESD), known as a framework of holistic school development (Bakirtzis 2004). Tony Shallcross's particularly perceptive view links change in education (and in ways of thinking and acting) with moral commitment, participatory and democratic functioning and co-operativeness in schools (given that the several groups share a common moral commitment for the general good). He compares this last element to the collectivity of the community and consequently to the influence that can be exerted on the school by an external factor. Shallcross links change with the concepts of self-regulation and interrelation. In his words,

> In educational contexts this conception of change is concerned with design and aspiration rather than planning and targets. Design and aspiration are open, organic, participative and iterative while planning and targeting are specific, mechanistic, controlling and time bound. In self-regulating systems change requires a trust in the processes of collaborative learning that may be incomplete but is informed by visions that have a few key priorities and structures. There are no single solutions. Pathways to success are virtually unknowable in advance of doing

something, so schools have to craft their own actions by being criti-cally reflective producers of change. This transformative, collaborative view of change shuns both individualism and collectivism in favour of interrelationalism. Individualism is inappropriate in school develop-ment because of its inherent self-interest and its implicit isolation of people as decision-makers. Collectivism is also irrelevant because it implies that individuals have no power, a view that sits uneasily with liberal notions of freedom. Interrelationalism is not a wet, reformatory compromise because unlike individualism and collectivism it is less concerned with outcomes than with the processes behind them, which is consistent with a whole school process-focused concept of EE/ESD. While the value of individualism and collectivism lies respectively with the individual or the collective, the value in interrelationalism is in the *relationships* between people.

(Shallcross, Robinson, Pace,
Wals & Bezzina 2006: 66–67)

This relation with others, this mutual coordination, articulates the intra-psychic with the interpsychic through affective response – that is through the emotional experience it provokes. In earlier periods, as we know, intel-lectuals like John Dewey, Francis Parker and Helen Parkhurst (Dalton Plan/ projects) stressed the role of life experience in learning (Tsoukala 2000). In the context of those views, however, life experience referred exclusively to the individual functions of the pupil beyond any plane of communica-tion and collaboration with other people. Later, the appearance of social psychology and the sciences of communication influenced educational research, orienting it towards the phenomena of group dynamics. This term became associated with the names of Kurt Lewin and later Karl Rogers (Bakirtzis 1996). Relational-centred education pushed aside discussions of pupil-centred and teacher-centred education, shifting the centre of gravity of educational practice to the communicational and interactive function of the members of the school community. The contribution of educational pioneers in the application of this model, and in the rethinking of the theoreticians who introduced the model, has been decisive. I shall mention in this regard the politicised educational science of Celestin Freinet (with Marxist influ-ences) and the institutional education movement (more complex in its objec-tives, with influences from Marxism, psychoanalysis and self-management) (Bakirtzis 2004: 164).

In Greece, Christos Fragos, who played an essential and pioneering role in contemporary education theory, creating in the universities of Ioan-nina and Thessaloniki a laboratory environment which fostered some very important researchers into the educational topics we are concerned with, has proposed an interesting dialectical teaching model. Fragos focuses on communication and dynamic interaction among the members of the school community. His Marxist approach incorporates elements of the Socratic method and underlines the role of collaboration and clash in the processes of learning and education.

This relational-centred current in education approaches the interpersonal dynamic from the aspect of the emotional involvement of the developing individual with his natural and cultural environment. Bakirtzis writes in his book *Communication and Education* that the concept of involvement refers to those conditions in which an individual, voluntarily or otherwise, concentrates emotionally, intellectually and/or bodily on a thought, idea, plan, action, activity, situation, person, group, object, phenomenon (Bakirtzis 2004: 309), and goes on to say that this concept of *involvement* refers to the interior experience that is characterised by self-concentration, intense experience, internal stimuli, energy flow, a high degree of satisfaction, contact with the emergence of a creative impulse leading to the integral engagement of the person and full activation of his abilities (Bakirtzis 2004: 312). In some earlier research of mine in France, one thing that emerged from analysis of the material garnered from the study of pupils of Freinet elementary schools was the importance of the involvement of place in the objectives of the school activities. This experiential relation between child and place contributes to the cultivation of a sense of responsibility for the action environment. At that time I had called this involvement *strategic spatial activity* so as to demonstrate the integration/inclusion of the space in the objects of the child's activity in a school environment (Tsoukala 2006, 2009). And I differentiated it from *passive spatial activity*, a term that rendered the limiting role of space to a form of life-container. With *strategic spatial activity* Freinet's educational system got children involved with their spatial environment, resulting in the emotional involvement and life experience that are essential conditions for the development of responsibility towards the child's material action environment, knowledge and assimilation. Consequently, the involvement of space in the child's activities – that is his involvement in its organisation, operation and aesthetic – led to his active engagement in matters of responsibility for the environment and the development of cognitive processes, especially in cases where the school space was itself a source of information about material (textures, materials, colour, light), science and technology (green schools, passive energy design, construction) and culture (syntax and grammar of the space). Today, when education is intensifying its research into the role of the environment in learning and education processes, the question of life experience and the emotional experience of space brings together specialists from many different disciplines involved with educational matters – teaching, psychology, social psychology, architecture. The material environment of the school should be a place where vivid experiences awaken and stimulate children's desires, motivations and interests, with the object of developing and cultivating their mental, emotional and social powers.

2 The architecture of educational modality
Qualities of space

As part of a society's cultural production, space functions as a sign, unlocking codes for its values, objects, orientations and concerns, representing at times the dominant currents and at others isolated trends acting in the backwash of the first. The focus of these paragraphs is on the impact of educational science and perceptions of learning on the organisation of the school environment's form and space. What emerges from the study of the evolution of educational views and theories is the spatial diffusion of the learning that is not immured within the material and educational confines of the classroom, but occurs throughout the whole school environment and that of the city, town or village in which it is located. Even when the demarcation of educational spatial units is an element of the planning, these have no sovereign role in the global school environment, but are treated as equal and equivalent to the public spaces in which the members of the school community move and act.

The term 'learning landscape', proposed by Hertzberger (2008), captures this perception of the spatial diffusion of learning, encapsulating the view that freedom of movement and exposure to a wealth and diversity of stimuli cultivate curiosity in the young, an appetite for and a disposition towards knowledge, discovery, invention and creation. This takes place within an intersubjective oscillation of school experience whose fixed point is the urban condition, the organised or random meetings of its inhabitants in the streets and squares and open public space of the city generally, programmed movements and idle saunterings among the exhibits of space and time. These qualities of urban space become, for many architects, a model for the architecture of school environments, not all of whom are successful, however, in transposing them to the much smaller-scale locus of educational activity, with its limited population and confined space. By the middle of the twentieth century the school-as-city was the primary model for school architecture, but in most cases it was limited to figural references to *urban artefacts* (we have borrowed the term from Aldo Rossi, who used it in *The Architecture of the City* [1981] to describe the timeless archetypical elements that make up a cityscape). Rossi conceives this way of considering urban space featuring its archetypical forms, and in designing a school in Fagnano Olona (a town in Northern Italy) resolves it morphologically and typologically on the basis of its theoretical constructs. Adhering rigorously to his urban facts and localised in the continuity of their typological forms and surfaces, he does not slip into a creative re-interpretation of their socio-temporal qualities. The haunting reference to the clock tower in the town square and its creative association with the stopped time of the souvenir photographs of childhood stress the symbolic dimension of the 'school-as-city', while its communicational-social dimension remains reduced and unexploited. Leon Krier (1998) follows the same symbolic logic in his design for the school at St Quentin-en-Yvelines, in France. These projects unquestionably display a disposition to de-institutionalise the school, expanding it beyond the walls of classroom and corridor, but they do not quite manage to exercise the power of architectural tools for creative re-interpretations of spatio-social concepts that a whole city offers. Such creative re-interpretations are exemplified in the work of the Dutch architect Hertzberger, the German Behnisch and the Catalan Miralles. The construction of intersubjective space, of encounters, meetings, dialogical and polyphonic co-existence, of rich social/learning interactions and exchanges – in other words, the substance of communicational action within the city – is what distinguishes the designs of these three architects, who consciously avoid alien architectural strategies imprisoned in imagined models and rigid principles.

The foregoing examples shed some light on the quality of 'dialogical/ polyphonic space' that we will be considering in the following pages, along with two other qualities of space – namely 'activated space' and 'playful space'. 'Activated space' is a quality we have proposed in earlier studies (Tsoukala 2001, 2007). As a concept it expresses the involvement of space in educational practice within a collaborative situation (contributing to the cultivation of responsibility, collegiality and environmental awareness). 'Playful space' is associated with *homo ludens* (Huizinga 2010) – that is with the free, voluntary physical and mental activity that cuts across our monotonous everyday routine and from which can emerge the 'subversive' event, the moment of rupture in the symbolic order, the point of creative intervention and change in the strangling network of cultural signs. We will begin with activated space, because we think that the question of the involvement of space in educational activities has acquired particular importance today in the context of the debate on environmental awareness and knowledge.

Before we begin, let us bring to mind the first attempt to de-institutionalise educational space on the basis of its character as dwelling-place. This concept lay behind an initial attempt to deschool the traditional teacher-centred educational environment and convert it into a place for experiencing life, a place of active participation within a familiar spatio-social framework. The classroom with all its teaching connotations was transformed into a dwelling-place, the rules relaxed in favour of the development of initiatives, encouraging the children to participate and engage creatively in the learning processes. Scharoun's schools (Blundell Jones 2000) are exceptional examples of this concept, their expressionistic style reinforced by the notion of the dwelling-place, which as a safe haven of free human corporeity and spirituality escapes the inflexibility of Euclidian logic, incorporating in its lines and surfaces emotions, desires, imagination – crucial structural elements of creative thinking and learning.

Quality 1: activated space

When I began to investigate the interrelation of space-perception-appropriation in different educational contexts (traditional and active/new education), and from a scientific point of view that put the social element at the heart of the overall consideration of the question, I realised that the involvement of space in the aims of the child's educational activity played an important role in the quality and intensity of the child-space relation. This involvement presupposed the 'flexibility and variability' of the space, the possibility of change in response to the needs and initiatives of the child assuming, responsibly, a role as a member of a community, a role that is connected with the organisation and arrangement of the space. This space I described then as 'activated', to distinguish it from the space that is simply equipped with the technical possibility of variability for its adaptation to the new external (as regards the child) operating conditions of that space. In addition to its technical/technological and psychological quality (in the case of the responsiveness of space in Piaget's and Moore's concept, with the child-space relation confined to the child's sensorimotor actions), the term 'activated' space carries a charged social aspect, since it connects the child's spatial behaviour with a collaborative educational framework, within which it is constructed[1] – a framework upon which Vygotsky laid particular emphasis when he investigated the role of cultural symbols (and primarily language) in human development and the influence of communication on the child's cognitive-learning function, which he ascribed to the zone of proximal development (Vygotsky 1934/1997; Doise & Mugny 1981). This difference in approach between the two great luminaries of that age, Piaget and Vygotsky, is clearly reflected in their correspondence on the subject (Clot 1999). For Vygotsky egocentric language is a transitional stage in the evolution from external to internal speech, while for Piaget it is a by-product of the child's activity, more closely resembling the logic of dreams than that of realistic thinking. That is the role of the social factor in the early stages of development (up to the seventh year) is given small value in Piaget: the biological element outweighs the social. Vygotsky, by contrast, links internal speech with the 'external' social environment, the child's social cultural experience, arguing the historical character of linguistically articulated meaning.

The social element involved in the processes of spatial perception in our experiments (Freinet's schools/child-centred education) seems to play an essential role in the construction of the child's image of space and himself. The assumption of responsibility within the context of a group for the smooth operation and organisation of a school space/area reinforces the 'identity' of the space and consequently the spatial perception process by which spatial elements and relations are recognised and acquire meaning. The deliberate character of the child's spatial awareness shows that the spatial representational phenomenon exists within the social-practical correlation of the child with the space in question. This spatial modality of awareness emerges precisely in the experience of responsibility and constitutes first responsibility and afterwards intentionality (Renaut 2009: 54). It constitutes responsibility towards the others: that is the child-subject does not remain enclosed within himself, but 'opens out' to the space-object and the other. Through this opening to the latter (to the other, in our case the collective other) he expands the space of his awareness. In pedagogical practice this builds up the child's awareness as an individual and a member of a collectivity and his recognition that his decisions are co-responsible for the orientation of the social-educational-spatial practices. Space as a structural element of social practice (and not as an inert or intelligent shell) participates in the construction of a responsible, enterprising subject whose individual action 'opens out' to a collectivity, is built on collective ties. The definition of *activated space* can be rendered with the following phrase: the organic social-educational involvement of space in the activities of the child, which leads to transformations of the space both on the material-practical and on the symbolic-conceptive level, influencing the structure of the child's consciousness. *Activated space* is not self-referential and is not confined to a dialectical relation with the corporeity of the subject. It is implicated in the social course of human history.

Of course, this approach does not take account of the psychoanalytical factor that revolutionised philosophy and all the disciplines of the humanities. Recognition of the structural non-identity of the subject 'shows that what the subject expresses consciously and defines the order of a conscious discourse always reveals primordial mental events that betray unconscious intentions and desires' (Lipovats & Romanos 2002: 25). Consequently, reflecting on the child's perception of space cannot ignore what Freud calls the 'philosophy of repression', which concerns the pathway of thought that arrives at awareness as a 'return of the repressed' (unfulfilled desires that have been expelled from the conscious and penetrate it in disguise) (Renaut 2009: 150). Nor can it ignore what Lacan, because he considers it incapable of rediscovering its lost/impossible real fulfilment in symbolic creation or imaginary representation, calls the deficient subject (Lipovats & Romanos 2002: 111). Contemporary reflections on the phenomenon of perception take into account the split that is characteristic of the human condition and lead to a redefinition of the relation of the subject with his environment. In this relation corporeity assumes different dimensions from those we described in the context of the approaches of Piaget and Vygotsky. Going beyond the boundaries of the sensorimotor-operational in the case of Piaget and the social/intentional/moral (responsible)-sensory-functional in the case of Vygotsky, psychoanalytical views promote graphic performative bodily action as the agent of a possible breach in the symbolic-alienative through the emergence and expression of desires towards the autonomy of the subject (different from its Kantian conception as modernity). This form of expression and inhabitation of the corporeal signalises *playful, fluid* and *empty* space, spatial concepts introduced by the post-structuralist visions of architecture, as we shall see in greater detail in the sections that follow.

Quality 2: dialogical-polyphonic space

Working in the same place and time as Vygotsky but in a different environment, Bakhtin (Emerson 1983; Pesic & Baucal 1996) reworked his dialogical theory in a study of techniques of composition and modalities of thought in the works of Dostoevsky. In his novels Dostoevsky handles a great diversity of material, and as Bakhtin says,

> If viewed from a monologic understanding of the unity of style, Dostoevsky's novel is multi-styled or styleless; if viewed from a monologic understanding of tone, Dostoevsky's novel is multi-accented and contradictory in its values. . . . The utterly incompatible elements comprising Dostoevsky's material are distributed among several worlds and several autonomous consciousnesses; they are presented not in a single field of vision (*that of the all-seeing author*[2]) but within several fields of vision . . . these worlds, these consciousnesses with their individual fields of vision [that] combine in a higher unity, . . . the unity of the polyphonic novel.
>
> (Bakhtin 1929/2000: 26–27)

It is thanks to this multiplicity of worlds that the novelist can develop to the utmost the varied otherness of his material without fragmenting or rendering mechanical the unity of the whole – a whole that is eternally moulded without ever crystallising into a final shape.

Bakhtin (who was belatedly made known to the West through the work, initially, of Kristeva and Todorov, and later by Jean Lods and Andrew Bennett, in the domain of literary criticism) views the individual not as an established authentic source of meaning but as an intersubjective dimension in which meaning is composed contrapuntally by different internal and external voices in a specific historical-social context. Undermining the closed integral polarity of self and other, he also militates against fragmentation and the dissolution of the subject, charging morality with the primary concern for the other. Steadfast recognition of different voices results in awareness of boundaries, activating the possibility of relocating them and opening new modalities of freedom.

To summarise this brief outline of the difference between Lacan and Bakhtin/Vygotsky, one might say that while for the former the removal of alterity is achieved through approximation to the *void* – we refer to the *event* as defined by Badiou (2008) and is situated at the 'edge of the void' – for the others it is achieved through the dialogical confrontational exchange that is situated on the social-symbolic level (which does not define an invariable framework of constant meaning but a suspended plexus of potentialities of unlimited sequences of contexts, signifiers and meanings). Standing opposed to Lacan's *Real* (the site of the deficiency, the void) is the *Symbolic-Communicational-Dialogical*, which is not accounted as an absolute datum but is constitutionally and conditionally bound up dialectically with each several social formation.

If architectural space is not to degenerate to the level of utilisation and fetishisation, to make its own contribution to the *alienation* of the subject through its monological nature and a spatial *pseudo-activity*, it must seek *dialogical* forms in the making.

A space that is designed and produced as a non-negotiated entity, however technically perfect on the level of the self-determining core of the symbolic order, is separate from and foreign to the subject and has an alienating effect. The subject is deprived of transformational possibilities within a single process that encloses subjective and objective elements, individual and social. He is displaced from the very material framework of his life (and from his broader environment), which is regulated by rules of a symbolic 'external' order (external as towards the subject since he has scarcely a hint of participation in the core of the productive-institutional-ruling processes and remains a passive individual moving peripherally and externally to it). In this situation the subject functions as an alienated entity, an offprint of the social 'deficit'.

Participatory design and open-ended design, which were much discussed in the context of the anthropology and psychosociology of space from the 1950s to the 1970s, express a kind of polyphonic architecture, but one still without the qualities of dialogical space. Those explorings placed the person at the centre of the process of producing space, removing from the architect-auteur the role of absolute regulator and owner of the project. These trends, which were represented Ralph Erskine, Giancarlo de Carlo, Peter and Alison Smithson, Shadrach Woods, Amos Rapoport, Roger Hart, Henry Sanoff, Gary Moore and others (the last three were concerned exclusively with school environments), are seen as forerunners of today's trends towards unfinished and fluid design and participatory software (in the field of digital-potential architecture). Naturally, the origin of these last includes more radical and anarchical architectural movements, such as the utopian proposals of Cedric Price and Constant, Super Studio, Archizoom and Archigram. Nonetheless, dialogical space is something more than participatory, neutral and open-ended design or Richard Llewelyn Davis's 'endless architecture'.[3] It is the space that incites the individual to a constant, fluid engagement with it and stimulates creative transformational intensities and dynamic/potential shifts on the dual level of its use and interpretation.

In contemporary architecture, line, constantly displaced as regards its initial form in relation to the ground, its adjacency to other lines and to the spectator/optical-neural inhabitant of the space, creates forms that 'stand constantly on the verge'. This sliding of form unbinds the sense of permanency, sweeps away meaning and shifts architecture from canonically combinative to suspended interpretation. The horizon of meaning is devised from the meeting of the lines with the ground/locus; it is not fixed, because this meeting is 'eternally recommencing'. With their suspended 'motion' the lines escape from objective universal laws and transcend time, dramatically juxtaposing their polyphonic semantic material.

The fluid emptiness of space replies to the question of the spatial expression of the dialogical condition, as does the irregularly labyrinthine space that invites not to an architectural promenade but to a perambulation through space offering a unique bodily coordinated experience exposed to stimulating potential encounters with the other. Through these meetings the self and its spatial situation are reconstructed. We will return to these topics of the conversion of dialogicality into characteristics of space in the third chapter of this book.

Another means of release from established symbolisms and fetishisms is provided by recourse to the imagination, which with admirable flexibility renders a variety of meanings in a single signifier. This leads to a weakening of the monological relation between signifier and signified. Wittgenstein's word games, the situationists' hijacking of meaning (*détournement du sens*), move within this logic of escape from the power of the signifier. 'Playful space', the third quality that we propose for a learning environment, has to do with those considerations. We shall look more closely in the following pages at the importance and role of this quality of space in the processes of a child's learning and socialisation.

Quality 3: playful space

Play protects us from excessive exposure to rules and symbols. Through play the child refracts the signified and familiarises himself with reality without the weight and the constraints of the symbolic order. Play as a phenomenon of human behaviour has been studied from many points of view, scientific and epistemic. Whether they come from psychology and psychoanalysis or from sociology and cultural anthropology, these studies agree on certain properties and characteristics of play. All play is a voluntary activity which obeys rules while allowing freedom of moves. Play is unpredictable as regards its evolution and ending because it is based to a degree on the freedom of the individual to invent and shape its continuation (Germanos 2004: 58). Also, it is associated with cheerfulness and enjoyment and resides in the world of the imagination. Imagination enables the child to turn meanings around, 'overcoming' the limitations imposed by the external objective conditions, and in that way, through the imagined overcoming of prohibitions, to 'satisfy' his deeper needs and desires. We must not forget, however, that in the case of the child the imagination plays a double role: it relieves him from the burden and bondage of the symbolic order and at the same time opens channels for him to accept it and make his co-existence with the other acceptable (preservation of the symbolic cohesion of the subject).

In contemporary theories of architecture the concept of play has been linked with the concept of drifting in space, which is the path of desymbolisation and freedom (Sadler 1998; Quentin 2007). Released from aims, programmed situations and externally guided actions, people move through the labyrinth of the city, experiencing in its unknown and unfamiliar areas the tensions caused by the foreign and the unexpected. Urban space as a playing field for the mental acrobatics of the surrealists and contemporary post-structuralists is built up as an imponderable life experience, as emerging events of spasmodic intensity and subversion, as self-directed and aimless actions of flâneurs in a world of liberty and creative bustle. From the *Cadavre Exquis* of Marcel Duhamel, Jacques Prévert and Yves Tanguy, Louis Aragon's *Paysan de Paris* and André Breton's *Nadja* to Coop Himmelblau's *Restless Ball* and Jean Dubuffet's *Jardin d'Email*, space emerges from the automatic writing, the fragmentary and random stitching together of mnemic situations, enjoyable experiences, cheerful and creative events (Lefaivre & Döll ab 2007) – a space-collage that contrasts with the ordered and externally determined space of programmed design and functional constraints. In this passionate journey beyond the commitments and the routine of everyday life, freedom and desire constitute the circumstances within which corporeal experiences unfold. Activities are continually constructed and reconstructed through the provocative and restless fluidity of the spatio-temporal stage – a provocation and invitation to experimental, newly emerging situations, subversive attitudes.

Architects invent various techniques, such as the blurring of the boundaries between discrete elements (between building and ground, between floor/wall and ceiling, between inside and out, and so on). These architectural treatments create a space without hierarchies and pre-designed directions, and stir up spatial images and attitudes provoking drifting and sometimes reversals. Classical ways of conceiving form through a re-interpretation of elements of the environment or recourse to mythical worlds can also convert the school building, or part of it, into objects of play (we shall go more deeply into these questions in Chapter 3).

The three qualities of school space that we have outlined here describe the intersection of pedagogy and architecture, the intersection of material man-made space with the contemporary condition of a stimulative, participatory, experiential learning. *Dialogical space* and *playful space* place the emphasis on open-ended, unbounded, coming-into-being space, on the fluidity – material and conceptual/symbolic – of space, while *activated space* declares the intentional involvement of space in the child's activities within a collaborative school life situation. These qualities translate into specific modalities of space, such as *flexibility*, *variability* and *interactivity*, the *labyrinthine organisation* of space and *fluid spatiality*, and, finally, *breadth of form*, *multiplicity*, *fluidity* and *transcending boundaries*. We consider these modalities to be directly linked with the qualities we have proposed. In the following chapters we shall go into them in greater detail.

Notes

1 I shall cite an example from research of mine in school environments in France (Tsoukala 2007), conducted at a time when I was interested in questions of the child's perception of space and how these could renew and enrich architectural design. Following Vygotsky's thinking, I considered the child, the building and the social environment of the school as a single interactive process rather than as different and independent elements, and studied the child in the specific spatial and pedagogical/educational environment. I selected two types of school space, *traditional* (classrooms arranged in series along a corridor) and *open* (free plan), and then associated each of the two types with two categories of pedagogical

activity, traditional (teacher-centred) and modern (child-centred/communicational model).

Here I shall refer to the case of the traditional school building combined with both traditional teacher-centred and collaborative pedagogy. The traditional school building globally shapes the values and models of guided teacher-centred pedagogy, which considers the individual as a passive recipient of the messages of the environment. Spatial activity in the framework of such a pedagogy degenerates into mere utilisation of the space, depriving the child of any possibility of altering its original meaning and adapting the space to his real needs. The symbolism of the space reinforces the message of the teaching practice and, alienated from the needs of the child, places him in an unfamiliar and disinterested world, in an isotropic space, in the space of the Other.

When the same school building functions on the basis of collaborative pedagogic practice, the symbolism, the signifier, is retained but the meaning is continually shifting. This is due to the kind of pedagogy which in its values proclaims group/collaborative work, the unity of theory and practice, and the integration of the material space itself into the school activities. This last I have called *spatial strategic activity*, and I have, through an analysis of the material, demonstrated its role in the mental and material appropriation of the space. The symbol, then, is weakened by the conversion of its meaning which occurs with a pedagogic practice that is collaborative in nature and expressed in an active *potential* space-child *relation* (spatial strategic activity). Here it must be stressed that spatial strategic activity presupposes the collaborative social relation that develops among the children during that activity. In the case of spatial activity we have, then, a double interactive relationship: with the space itself and with the other. The traditional school building is transformed by the new pedagogic condition into a familiar place, anything but alien to the child. From an institution it has become a life-space. This example illustrates the strength of pedagogical spatial practice in the transformational process of giving meaning to space. This process could be supported (facilitated) by the characteristics of the space itself. In our example the elements of its space had a discouraging permanency. But the equipment within it was movable, enabling changes to be made in the organisation of the classrooms (re-arranging the furniture to facilitate collaborative group work) and the school's public spaces to suit the logic and the values of the pedagogic method.

2 My insertion and emphasis.
3 In a lecture to the AA in London Davis described Mies's Alumni Memorial Hall as endless architecture, an allusion to James Joyce (see Lucan 2010).

3 From qualities to modalities

Modality 1: flexibility, transformability, interactivity

Space considered as a demarcated void is a topic that has been extensively explored from the aspect of both style and content. Depending on the period it has been associated with rigid typologies and, conversely, with provocative spatial continuities. Compartmentalised and absolutely predetermined in its uses in the first case; in the second, a changeable and hospitable pocket of time, unified and wholly coordinated in a succession of moments and needs. Depending on the period, it bears the imprint of time either frozen and invariable or rhythmic in repetitions of spatial elements and the fluctuating intensities of the resulting combinations. Sometimes, too, time appeared as the dominant element in its interaction with space, subjecting it to its interminable flow.

It was modern architecture, giving voice to the great and rapid changes of the industrial age, that first raised the question of flexibility and spatial continuity. Together with the concept of functionality that refers literally and metaphorically to the machine, *flexibility* is the quality that gives a more fluid and variable character to the interior of an otherwise austere, spare and orthonormal construction. In most projects the contained space is defined by its spatial continuity, a motif beloved of modern architects and supremely exemplified by Mies van der Rohe's Barcelona Pavilion, where freely spaced horizontal and vertical planes create an intriguing spatiality and relationship with the surrounding area. Flexibility and spatial continuity are, of course, two different concepts. Spatial continuity describes a space with freely communicating areas, without boundaries – transparent or movable – to block the flow of physical movement and spatial experience. Flexibility refers mainly to the ability of the space to change and adapt as required by the inhabitant. This is achieved through the use of movable partitions to divide or unify the space, depending on their position. One example is Rietveld's *Schröder* house, with its characteristic sliding panels on the upper storey to provide more or less privacy, as desired. Another is Erskin's *Box* house, with a movable platform that was lowered to the floor at night to provide a sleeping area and raised to the ceiling at other times to free the floor space. It is precisely this form of flexible space that we find in school buildings of the inter-war period (and afterwards), designed to allow rooms to be thrown together or partitioned into smaller areas according to teaching requirements for group work. It could be argued that even the shell of a building displays flexibility, since the movable (sliding/hinged or folding) surfaces on its façade separate or unify the interior and exterior space. This feeling is particularly strong when a closed space is converted into a semi-outdoor area by removing one side of the shell, allowing, in single-storey buildings, the educational activities to spill out into the open-air space around them. This was a flexibility dictated in the inter-war period by the new education movement, as well as by health regulations to improve spatial living conditions. The tenets of this twofold thrust led to the development of numerous types of single-storey school buildings designed to achieve optimum orientation, light and ventilation as well as an immediate relation with the natural or urban setting (Tsoukala 2000).

Another outstanding example of inter-war architecture, the Antonio Sant'Elia nursery school in Como, Northern Italy, designed by Giuseppe Terragni (Terragni, Libeskid & Rosselli 2004), has a plastic interior spatiality created by the door-walls and furniture-walls that organise the divisions of its contained space, allowing for great flexibility of use, while the transparency that is the most striking feature of its shell (sliding floor-to-ceiling-glass windows) creates a sense of there being no boundaries between the school's interior and the exterior space.

Eliminating the material boundary between interior and exterior space was the object of open-air schools designed along the lines of sanatoria as a health measure. In *Trends in School Architecture* we mentioned that the pavilion plan was proposed by doctors (and later associated with the arrangement of classrooms in wings, on the finger plan, and with the idea of the classroom as living-space). The open-air school built by Marcel Lods and Eugène Beaudouin in Suresnes in 1935, five years after Duiker's open-air school in Amsterdam (Hertzberger 2000), is an example of the pavilion type which features units limited essentially to a roof: they function, in other words, as one with the natural setting since on three sides (south, east and west) the walls can be left open or closed, with only the north wall remaining fixed (Figures 3.1a–b). Other examples of open-air school buildings with similarly flexible walls are the school designed by Richard Neutra in Los Angeles and the Impington Village School in Cambridgeshire (1939), designed by Gropius and Fry (Boesiger 1964; Reginald 1983) (Figures 3.2a–b).

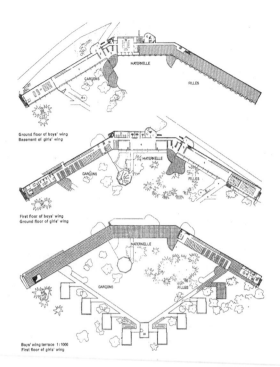

Figure 3.1a School complex in Suresnes (1935–36). Architects: Lods & Beaudouin.
Floor plans.

Source: Hertzberger, H. (2000). *Space and the Architect: Lessons in Architecture 2*. Rotterdam:
nai010: p. 55, f. 85; p. 56, f. 89.

Figure 3.1b School complex in Suresnes (1935–36). The classroom-pavilion.

Source: Hertzberger, H. (2000). *Space and the Architect: Lessons in Architecture 2*. Rotterdam:
nai010: p. 55, f. 85; p. 56, f. 89.

Figure 3.2a Corona School in Los Angeles (1935). Architect: R. Neutra. Classrooms.

Source: Boesiger, W. (ed.) (1964). *Richard Neutra 1923–50: Buildings and Projects*, introduction by S. Giedion. Zurich: Verlag fur Architektur: p. 153.

Figure 3.2b Impington Hall in Cambridgeshire (1936). Architects: W. Gropius & M. Fry. Classrooms.

Source: Reginald, I. (1983). *Gropius: An Illustrated Biography of the Creator of the Bauhaus*. London: Bulfinch Press Book: p. 209.

Flexibility of interior space in school buildings became a priority in the period immediately after the Second World War. Open-plan schools (the type was developed in response to a combination of financial and pedagogical considerations) are characterised by spatial continuity, flexible space (Bennett, Andreae, Hegarty & Wade 1980). The use of sliding partitions and movable equipment served the new methods of differentiated instruction within a framework encouraging the pupils to engage in free, self-initiated, creative activity. Open-plan schools reflected this teaching practice, transposing that classroom organisation to the scale of the entire building after the changes introduced by the theories of physicians, such as Maria Montessori and Ovide Decroly. The Amersham School built in 1950 was the first example of a semi-open design in England. That school had eight classrooms organised in two groups of four in a way that permitted direct communication between them without the interposition of a corridor. From then on flexibility became the keyword in designing school buildings. Another two noteworthy examples with characteristically flexible floor plans are the Finmere School in Oxfordshire and the Lowe Eveline Primary School in London's Southwark. Open-plan design dominated school construction in England throughout the 1960s, and by the end of that decade had become an international phenomenon.

In Greece, Zenetos began to design a junior school for the south-eastern suburb of Aghios Dimitrios, Athens (Kalafati & Papalexopoulos 2006), in 1969; the plans were completed in 1972. With louvred roofs accenting its perfectly circular shape, it is one of the most interesting examples of school architecture of its era, not only for its interior flexibility, which goes beyond mere adaptability to future functional requirements, but also as a proposal for the pedagogical qualities of the future school and the future communication and information society. The plans propose three stages of operation, taking account of contemporary and future construction possibilities. In stage three the perimetric arrangement of separate classrooms is converted, together with the atrium, into a flowing, flexible space (the classrooms are eliminated and the walls replaced by light, movable partitions) with the 'teaching core' – that is the computers and multimedia – at its centre (Figure 3.3).

With today's post-structuralist approach to the organisation of space, the concepts of flexibility and spatial continuity are giving way to that of variability. As used in contemporary architecture, and particularly in its digital version, the term carries a sense of (spatio-temporal) change more radical than that associated with flexibility or spatial continuity. The current emphasis on the term is explained by the possibilities of electronic technology and contemporary materials technology, and by the theoretical epistemic concentration on the lived body, the 'intelligent' body that thinks, desires and interacts with its

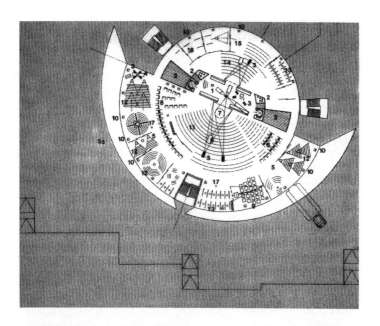

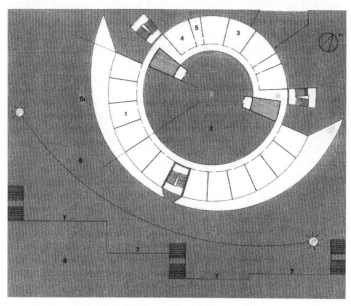

Figure 3.3 Aghios Dimitrios Gymnasium-Lyceum, Athens (1969–1974). Design: Takis Zenetos. Ground plan of a typical floor in the school's first and third operating phase.

Source: Kalafati, E. & Papalexopoulos, D. (2006). *Takis X. Zenetos: Virtual Visions and Architecture*. Athens: Libro: p. 116, Floor plan A' Phase; p. 117, Floor Plan C' Phase. © Hellenic Institute of Architecture

environment. Fluidity or liquidity and responsiveness are the terms associated with variability, followed at a distance by flexibility (and spatial continuity).

Fluidity/liquidity permeates our whole contemporary culture and marks the period of globalisation, with unprecedented changes of speed and their consequences on the organisation of spatio-social life. Bauman (2007, 2008) uses it in the titles of two books: *Liquid Times*, subtitled *Living in an Age of Uncertainty*, and *Liquid Love: On the Frailty of Human Bonds*. As a sociologist Bauman examines the short life expectancy of social practices/ human bonds (liquidity-uncertainty), the factors that shape it and its consequence for man and modern societies. In architecture liquidity correlates primarily with the philosophical post-structuralist discourse that attributes the woes of the subject to the established symbols of the culture and the absence of that same subject (as mind and body/sense perception) from the scene of social life. This correlation leads to exaggerated emphasis on the positive role of the liquidity of signs that is achieved with the integration of bodily experience into the material of architecture. In this sense the materiality of the built constantly shifts its signifiers and by extension its meanings, aiming at the freedom of the individual, his disengagement from the order that is built in his absence. The inscription of bodily experience[1] into the material and in general the social formation does not refer here to the phenomenological formulation 'being-in-the-world', an expression conceptually woven from strands of identity, rootedness, locality. 'Being-within-the-world', by contrast, in the post-structuralist perception of the world tends towards the deconstruction of identity and the forging of a repertory of self-roles within the constantly shifting, variable and fuzzy boundaries of the signs. There are, naturally, different approaches to this perception, more or less critical, when we refer to specific cases of spatial organisation/social groups, such as that of a school. In this case *liquidity* is examined in relation to the age of the child (his need for fixed points of reference revises aspects of the post-structuralist approach and seeks new equilibria between liquidity and stability). Experiments with school buildings follow innovations in architectural composition, although often with a time lag, a delay that is due to the institutional character of their function, which seems to remain remote from developments on other levels of function of social forms.

Today, the term 'fluidity' or 'liquidity' is often used in conjunction with that of 'interactivity', which denotes the capacity of the material of the architectural project to change, to be transformed, acting as a new interface with the user depending on his needs and expectations. Early in the twentieth century this concept, contained in the term *responsiveness*, appears in the work of Jean Piaget (1947), who, studying with his associates the stages of child development, observed that a child's mental functions and understanding are reinforced in environments that have that property. He argued that a child is mentally stimulated when he interacts with the objects that he is manipulating, because the transformed object operates as a new stimulus, keeping the child's attention and interest unabated. This is a process involving all the senses, an observation which spurred Piaget to devise the term 'practical intelligence', to which he gave particular emphasis. A few decades later, when the modern movement was accused of using built space as a tool and many architects turned to the humanities as a source of ideas and elements for the qualities of inhabited space, the term responsiveness was added to the vocabulary of architectural idiom. We find it in studies of environmental psychology (or the psychology of space, as it was originally called) focusing on children's spatial perception and behaviour. Looking at the relation between cognitive/learning performance and space, Gary Moore (1987) and his associates in the School of Architecture at the University of Wisconsin–Milwaukee observed that the quality of the spatial and other elements to adapt to the action performed on them during the operation of the learning process had a positive effect on the child's cognitive processes and in general on his appropriation of space. This marks the first appearance of the concept of responsiveness on the scale of architectural space, and it is directly associated with its psychological qualities.

With today's advanced technologies this property of space as interactivity can now be achieved automatically if the building's digital surfaces are programmed to react in response to environmental messages. Desired levels of light or shade, temperature and so forth can be achieved thanks to digital technology, and playful shapes and forms that mark fleeting events emerge from the visualisation of moments of motion, sound and spatial density. Intelligent materials are programmed to have precise reactions to phenomena, resulting in observable changes in the form and function of architectural elements (Ouggrinis 2012). These self-adjusting surfaces provoke satisfaction, surprise, an awakening of the senses and keenness of observation, but do not stop acting exclusively as surfaces to be looked at. The child becomes the spectator of an *intelligent* construction, initially enigmatic but which rapidly loses its initial impressively iconoplastic availability to degenerate into an object with limited and almost demarcated functions – more challenging and stimulating perhaps than an invariable construction, but still alien to the child himself. We consider a construction interactive with the child when it is the child who moderates its changes, when he takes part actively in those changes, making it a *tool* for *learning-play-experience*. I am not the ideal person to enumerate the forms of active handling of hi-tech surfaces and spatial elements available to the child. What is important is that we understand the difference between a built environment that interacts with the persons who inhabit it on multiple levels and a built environment that reacts unilaterally in their

their movement or in objectively predetermined microclimatic environmental conditions.

The building as a tool for learning became an object of consideration in the context of educational theory around the middle of the twentieth century. Notional opposites, such as large/small, low/high, light/dark, open/closed, private/public, warm/cold, smooth/rough and hard/soft, and functions, like the circulation of water or electricity, drainage and heating systems, can be grasped through the architecture of the building. The effectiveness of different sizes and shapes in the rooms and their several elements, the use of different materials and visible power and plumbing networks, the presentation of those systems with the help of colours, and other strategies for the organisation of the building-as-learning-tool were used in schools in various parts of the world. This concept has been revived today with the need for environmental education in schools (Tsoukala & Voyatzaki 2004). In recent decades, the designing of school buildings has concentrated systematically on the question of energy. It is a problem that involves numerous disciplines in addition to architecture, and experts from many fields are brought into the planning team at the initial stage of developing the compositional idea. Questions relating to the energy behaviour of a building that could be object lessons in pre-school and school classrooms include the orientation of the building, the passive systems used to save energy, construction materials, colours, the mechanisms and systems that convert one form of energy into another in order to save electricity, and the whole subject of recycling (Figure 3.4). The wavy green strips roofing the Sembat High School in France and the Vilhelmsro Primary School in Denmark (designed respectively by Archi5 and BIGArchitects) exemplify this ecological logic in construction and (environmental) education, as does the Paul Chevalier complex in Rillieux-la-Pape (France), designed by Tectoniques.[2] Today this is supplemented by the self-adjusting or adjustable variability of building surfaces, a property that collaborates in the context both of its own environmental behaviour and of the environmental education of the child, or in the logic of the child's playful relation with the environment of his school life. This is illustrated by the experiments of the Baupiloten group at the University of Berlin, whose proposals include interventions in the exterior walls of school buildings that convert the 'corridors' into dynamic and variable spaces that can be used for a wide variety of activities, organised and informal. These surfaces function interactively with the children and adapt according to their needs and wishes (locker space, meeting area, relaxation, study space). The variability of the space and the moderating role of the child in the process make the shell itself and other elements of it into tools, inter-mediators between the child and the broader environment, or *psychological tools*, to use Vygotsky's term (Wertsch 1985)

Figure 3.4 Paul Chevalier school complex in Rillieux-la-Pape, Lyon (2013). Design: Tectoniques. View of part of the building.

Source: STUDIO Tectoniques' archive. © Photograph, STUDIO Tectoniques

for every sign that belongs to the system of codes of human culture and through its use participates in the construction of the image of the environment and the spatial experience.

Moving from the shell of the school building to its interior, where a wealth of social-educational activities, formal and impromptu, take place, we find variable hi-tech systems that offer a variety of alternative solutions on the level of equipment for learning areas and places where the entire school community gathers. The property of variability extends to the interior space, facilitating the educational process and advancing the educational goals relating to flexible practices and learning schemes, participation and initiative on the part of the child, adaptation to new conditions and experimentation.

Examples of this kind of variability based on movable and convertible equipment (furniture and partitions) that can be divided and recombined in many ways (to suit the needs and wishes of the children) are found in the Vittra schools in Sweden. Rosan Bosch (2013) worked with the Vittra International Schools to create new learning environments in the context of contemporary perceptions of learning and habitational space. Using new materials and technologies, Bosch designed a single through-flowing interior space containing 'sitting islands' for relaxation and informal communication, 'lunch clubs' for meals and group projects, an open construction in the form of an iceberg that replaces the traditional amphitheatre, and closed rooms for sound-insulation and security purposes. Shapes, colours and rapid transformations of the learning landscape made possible by the convertibility and recombinability of the spatial elements create a free and fluid environment for educational processes organised to serve the criteria of experience, collaboration, and voluntary and independent contact with knowledge. Bosch organises the space in such a way that despite its fluidity and variability the points and areas of soft flow and change predominate over those of greater intensity. This happens because she takes into account the fact that, in an educational environment especially, constant points of reference are essential for the child's mental and emotional reconstruction of the space. Kostis Oungrinis has worked along similar lines with his students in the School of Architecture at the Technical University of Crete. Recently, at a two-day seminar entitled 'Reshaping the Learning Environment in the Kindergartens in the Prefecture of Rethymno: Architectural Redesign and Educational Exploitation', organised by the Faculty of Education of the University of Crete in collaboration with the Technical University (25–26 May 2013), Oungrinis presented the results of these 'experiments': variable constructions that avoid established forms and symbolisms, treading a line between the fantastic and the real/functional.

Modality 2: liquidity, taut fluidity

There are architects who have explored ways of creating a rich *spatiality*, attractive and provocative, a spatiality opposed to the horizontal organisation of areas and the communication of spatial levels mediated by a staircase whose role is limited to up and down movement from one level to the other (Van Heuvel 1992; Lucan 2010; Scoffier 2011). Seen exclusively as an element of vertical traffic movement, the staircase belongs to the same category as the corridor, a simple spatial means of preplanned movement in space. Seen from a diametrically opposite point of view, however, the staircase is a dynamic element that pierces through each level and, displacing the compact elements of space, creates voids that set off its sculptural essence and determinant role in the matter of communication and spatio-social tensions. The *void* that is created acts as a social and mental condenser since the necessary meeting with the other, the different, the individual teacher or fellow pupil, larger or smaller, the world of the community, takes place in this empty space – a space of reception and exhibition, a space of meeting and contact, a space of rich experiences in an educational framework less prescribed than that of the teaching areas.

Proper design articulates the planes visually and functionally, and creates a spatio-temporal flow that passes through all the levels of the building, offering unorthodox perspectives and a transparency essential for contact among the inhabitants of the space in moments of relaxation, recreation and sociality, as well as for moments of exposure to the gaze of the other: exhibition space, where student work is displayed, theatrical space, where performances collect an audience, space for talks that demand participation in the discussions that follow, reflection on the unfolding of the discourse and the escalation of the arguments.

The *void* in architecture, as a space disengaged from signs and elements, has been re-assessed in the context of considerations of deconstructivist and post-structuralist architecture. Like Lacan's void, which corresponds to the potential element and to reversals of the moment, so empty space is the place in which potential acts can happen, the potential action of the students, bearer of the creative participative attitude in the context of the educational process. Empty space is not symbolised space. It is the place of the potential, the place of distance from the repetitive here and the cyclical now and their evolutionary history. In this sense empty space is not the phenomenological locus of the *Dasein*. The experience of the subject in empty space is different from Heidegger's experience of *being-within-the-world*, in the world of signs and boundaries. Potentialisation is the change of identity, the unexpected shift of the subject's ontological centre of gravity. And this shift can take place in empty undetermined space and in a field of communication and dialogue, in a field of imponderable multiplicity where interpersonal exteriority opens fertile breaches in human interiority.

In order to build this *void* architects looked to the work of Piranesi, the engravings of his oneiric labyrinthine spaces, utopian in the sense that they cannot be realised, that they leave the viewer with an unresolved perplexity, an invitation to redefine the space and its habitation. The void is folding longitudinally, emptying the space of its signs, creating transparency in favour of vision and communication, a space that displaces every punctual functionality, placing the reflective subject at its *empty* centre. This empty space establishes the synchronicity of events and episodes, intensifies intersubjectivity, creates an oppositional rather than a sequential order of spaces. Its vertiginous motion swallows up all meanings, turns time into moments and assigns to verticality the properties of the horizontal Dostoevskian world. The well-designed final monophonic function is replaced by the alterity of discourse, the multiplicity of voices and encounters, of words spoken and exchanged, of actions and interactions.

Architects turned not only to Piranesi but also to the Baroque, which countered religious division with the creation of a vigorous and intensely emotional spatiality which is produced by the pulsating mass with its perpetually refoldings. The division of space into parts and elements that obey strict rules of proportion and harmony no longer applies, nor does the logic of additive composition. Curving surfaces draw each separate element into their folds, making them part of a single mass whose pulsations define fluid single spaces in dynamic movement, open-ended in their tendency to approximate the infinity of the divine. The concept of spatiality is exemplified in truly extraordinary fashion in this period of architecture, which also penetrates the contemporary consideration of questions focusing on the coming-into-being of space, on surfaces that swallow up the boundaries/ divisions of space – natural and built – to shape a landscape that is continuous and non-discrete. In such a space opposites participate unhindered in the process of its synthesis without discordant clashings. Subjects coexist in the pulsating movement of its vital mass, which unfolds deliberately towards the divine in an attempt to stretch the spirit and redeem it from the material forces that are exercised on man.

The intent behind the folds in the built surface in contemporary architecture, and the resulting spatiality, is not to absorb clashes thanks to communication with a higher spiritual world but to abolish the major prioritised differences and to create a playful network of minor, diverse, amorphous differences that with their constant displacements and collisions shape a flowing, dynamic spatial field, with blurred boundaries and contours like those of the Impressionist painters.

We find an exciting, vibrant, fluid spatiality in the schools (in their interior, closed, public areas) designed by Herman Hertzberger, Günter Behnisch and Enric Miralles, and an exceptional example of climate-dictated semi-open-air spatiality in Bidinost's Escuela Manuel Belgrano in Cordoba, Argentina.

Hertzberger's schools are born of the structuralists' concern to stress spatial relations rather than the functional elements of space (van den Heuvel 1992). Transitions, with their socio-psychological and existentialist qualities, assume a leading role in the creation of an architecture of communication that is interested not in form but in the spatial folds that escalate empty spaces and their intensities, incorporating into its logic the individual functional elements. Suspended within the preponderating void are the closed teaching spaces (classrooms), while staircases and work balconies link the different levels, conducing to a labyrinthine, Piranesian, communicative atmosphere that invites contact and congregation. The adventuresome spatiality of mediaeval urban fabrics is creatively re-inscribed in the 'small city' of the school space, for, as he says in *Space and Learning*, 'every educational building calls for a spatial order that works as a structure of streets and squares together forming a small city where everything is geared to the greatest possible number of social contacts, confrontations, meetings, adventures and discoveries' (Hertzberger 2008: 123).

In the Apollo schools (1981–83) he proposed the organisation of learning areas around a central space, which, he argued, since children would automatically tend to congregate there, would afford more opportunities for accidental, spontaneous contacts between children of different ages. This space is organised amphitheatrically on two levels, increasing visual contact among its users (Figures 3.5a–b and 3.6). In Hertzberger's own words,

> Situations of players and audience arise easily and spontaneously: children sitting on the treads of the stairs connecting the two levels soon start behaving like an audience, thereby challenging the players on the lower level to give what you might call a performance.
>
> (Hertzberger 1991: 213)

Later, in the Montessori College Oost (Hertzberger 2000) in Amsterdam, this amphitheatrical space acquires Piranesian qualities with its interesting

Figure 3.5a Apollo schools in Amsterdam (1980). Design: H. Hertzberger. View of the central common space.

Source: Hertzberger, H. (1991). *Lessons for Students in Architectures.* Rotterdam: nai010: p. 215, f. 600; p. 215, f. 602; p. 213, f. 597–598. © Photograph, Johan van de Keuken

Figure 3.5b Apollo schools in Amsterdam. View of the central common space.

Source: Hertzberger, H. (1991). *Lessons for Students in Architectures*. Rotterdam: nai010: p. 215, f. 600; p. 215, f. 602; p. 213, f. 597–598. © Photograph, Johan van de Keuken

interplay of levels, perspectives and uses (Hertzberger 2000). This building is a richer interpretation of the city and its social and collective qualities compared to his earlier work in the Apollo schools. The city with its open public spaces, thresholds, intermediate transitional spaces, prospects, surprises and variegated construction is a source of qualities of space for the scale of the dwelling-place, and particularly for public buildings like schools. Spatial structure and form provide a stimulus for social contacts, rich encounters, chance meetings and behaviours. Through this sort of viewpoint Hertzberger concentrates his interest on the urban qualities of space, exploring every aspect of it as regards the way of provoking social collective behaviour within or outside the established frameworks of our co-existence

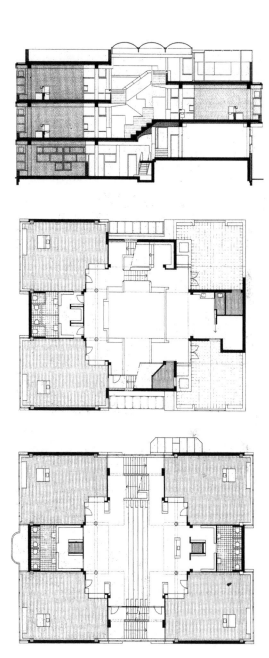

Figure 3.6 Apollo schools in Amsterdam (1980). Design: H. Hertzberger. Floor
plans and section.

Source: Hertzberger, H. (1991). *Lessons for Students in Architectures.* Rotterdam: nai010:
p. 215, f. 600; p. 215, f. 602; p. 213, f. 597–598. © Photograph, Johan van de Keuken. ©
Drawings, Herman Hertzberger

in the city, in a perspective of possible transformations. In the Montessori College Oost the boundaries between private (classrooms) and public space are preserved in a flexible spatial situation guaranteed by the autonomy of the structural bearing system (free-plan) and the use of light, movable partitions. What seems to absorb Hertzberger's entire effort to create a dialogical-polyphonic space is its public part, the social condenser where the boundaries of formal and informal activities merge, as do children of different ages, members of the school community and others. Ramps, work balconies hung at different heights that act as amphitheatres bridging the classroom wings, broad staircases, empty spaces and open galleries build up a vertically oriented public space, orchestrating social collective activities and behaviours. This fluid Piranesian spatiality articulates the geometrically disciplined classroom wings, dissolves any sense of a rigid and predetermined framework, central reference and ordering point. In this synchronic diverse landscape of actions and roles school life sheds its normative form and becomes an adventure (Figures 3.7 and 3.8).

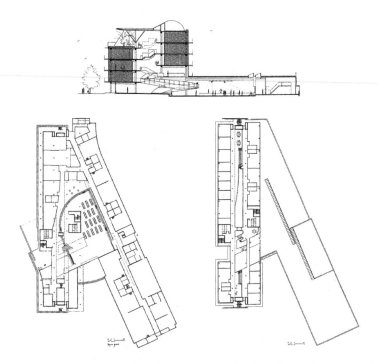

Figure 3.7 Montessori College Oost, Amsterdam (1999). Architect: H. Hertzberger. Floor plans and section.

Source: Hertzberger, H. (2000). *Space and the Architect: Lessons in Architecture 2*. Rotterdam: nai010: p. 170, f. 372A+B+C. © Drawings, Herman Hertzberger

Figure 3.8 Montessori College Oost, Amsterdam (1999). Architect: H. Hertzberger.
View of the central common space.

Source: Hertzberger, H. (2008). *Space and Learning: Lessons in Architecture 3*. Rotterdam:
nai010: p. 124, f. 2. © Photograph, Herman Hertzberger

The same spatiality, perhaps more conflictual than that of Herman Hertz-berger's buildings, is seen in the schools designed by Günter Behnisch, which are conceived in a curious equilibrium between a deconstructive and a rational spatial formation. As Peter Blundell Jones says, there is no 'Behnisch style', for he never developed one, but used a bewildering variety of forms (Blundell Jones 2000: 7). It is also very difficult to recognise the author of any of his projects, since the design process as practised by his firm was an open, collective proceeding, and the projects took shape in a dialogical working environment. Influenced by expressionist architects like Häring and Scharoun, he held that an oppressive geometrical discipline is incapable of expressing the diverse human psychological and existential reality. He linked free, open form with the freedom of the individual. Like Hugo Häring, he thought that forms should never impose themselves, but should be revealed through a non-prefigured process of inquiry and exposure to the unknown and momentary. In current terms (as used in post-structuralist architectural currents) this means that the interest has shifted from form to the process of producing it. Contributing to the translation of this idea on the bringing-forth of form into material reality was the concept of the 'layering of façades' that Behnisch borrowed from Mies and Eier-mann. The superposition and interplay of construction layers are reflected in the configuration of the exterior surfaces, creating a playful atmosphere. In the St Benno Grammar School in Dresden, the part that communicates with the urban element remains subject to its rules, while the rest decon-structs the orthonormal building logic, engaging with the free shapes of the natural environment. The interplay and conflict of opposing forms create a bold empty space that cuts across the levels of the building, unifying it visu-ally and functionally (Figures 3.9 and 3.10a–b). With the diagonal slope of the glass roof the environment penetrates into the interior of the building and vice versa. The interior of the building refuses privacy, betting on public-ity. Something similar can be seen in other school buildings he designed, such as the Albert Schweitzer Special School (1991) in Bad Rappenau (Fig-ure 3.11a–b), near Heilbronn (Blundell Jones 2000). For Behnisch, 'the goal of architectural work is not just the building but much more the situation to be created' (Blundell Jones 2000: 14).

The work of Enric Miralles is wholly unclassifiable – and this is con-firmed by everything he designed, without exception. The extension to the national youth school of music in Hamburg proposes a linear arrange-ment of spaces with flaring ends (one end being the existing building) and projections all along its length. In the calm severity of the urban fabric, this building fills the empty urban space not with a conflictual logic but with a playful and impertinent disposition. In this building the interior empty space is continually transformed, reacting to the pauses of the closed spaces (rooms) surrounding it. The void invites and challenges

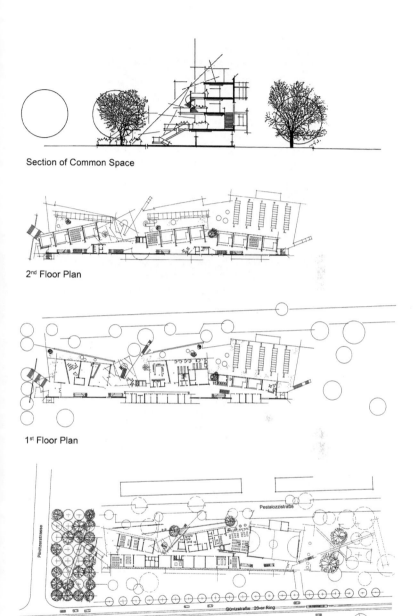

Section of Common Space

2nd Floor Plan

1st Floor Plan

Ground Floor Plan

Figure 3.9 St Benno School, Dresden (1996). Design: G. Behnisch. Floor plans and east façade.

Source: STUDIO Behnisch & Partners' archive. © Drawings, Behnisch & Partners

Figure 3.10a St Benno School. Interior common space.

Source: Blundell Jones, P. (2000). *Günter Behnisch*. Basel: Studio Paperback: p. 59, hall.
© Photograph, Christian Kandzia

Figure 3.10b St Benno School. Interior common space.

Source: Gauzin-Muller, D. (1997). *Behnisch & Partners: 50 Years of Architecture*. Berlin: Academy Editions: p. 263, the recreation space under construction. © Photograph, Christian Kandzia

Figure 3.11a Albert Schweitzer School in Bad Rappenau (1991). Architect: G. Behnisch. Ground floor plan and section.

Source: Gauzin-Muller, D. (1997). *Behnisch & Partners: 50 Years of Architecture*. Berlin: Academy Editions: p. 180, detail of hallway; p. 182, ground floor plan; p. 185, cross section.
© Photograph, Christian Kandzia

Figure 3.11b Albert Schweitzer School in Bad Rappenau (1991). Architect: G. Behnisch. Interior common space.

Source: Gauzin-Muller, D. (1997). *Behnisch & Partners: 50 Years of Architecture*. Berlin: Academy Editions: p. 180, detail of hallway; p. 182, ground floor plan; p. 185, cross section.
© Drawings, Behnisch & Partners

the inhabitant of the space to constant movement and action. Miscellaneous ramps and stairs cross it, insisting on the perpetual interaction and co-existence of people and events. The stairs, polytonic as regards their material (concrete and metal), form and colour, constructions fixed or playfully suspended in empty space, weave together with the other forms of movement in height, a labyrinthine tectonics that gives the building a fluid structurality. Multiple pathways and angles of vision intensify the fourth dimension of space, the temporal dimension, increasing the extent and duration of the social collective engagements. This dimension, which tormented Miralles, is realised by the immaterial void, by the emptying of the massive, by the synchronicity of the spatial episodes, by the exposure of discords. Space is experienced through the tensions of the accidental, the unexpected and unforeseen, through free bodily experience and the consequent social dialogical situation. Miralles's architecture is diversely polyphonic and hyper-expressive, on the cusp of myth and reality, of the timeless and the contemporary, of the unfinished and the open (Figures 3.12a–b, 3.13 and 3.14a–b). Each element constitutes a singularity that is constantly transformed, multiplying in pursuit of difference, not similarity, in allusion to the polytonality of the school community, the structure of knowledge and the self within a polyphonic, dialogical, interactive interpersonal environment (Miralles 2005). Its lines are constantly shifting, curling and unfolding, pulsating, describing fluid spaces not only within the interior void but also in the shell of the building, its borderline and polysemic encounter with the elements of its surrounding space (e.g. the displacements due to the trees on the front side). These continual transformations and reconstitutions of the spatial elements create a fragmentary image that contains within itself the force of disarticulation against permanent, integral and established meaning, offering a spatiality of the temporary and transient. The façades of brick, metal and glass, their colour reinforced by the playfulness of the building, beat to the rhythm of the trees, creating an interesting Baroque-type spatiality which slips into the interior of the school. Every line calls forth a different sentiment and emotion in the viewer, as do the different sounds of music or letters of the alphabet, depending on their combination and the meanings they express or wish to be released from. The polytonic spatiality Miralles created in this school, dynamic and flowing, carries in its fluidity impressions, emotions, games of the mind and the imagination, actions and reactions, in their most plural and heterogenous version. And here, as in his other works, the chorography of space draws us into a living adventure, a journey towards liberty of action and expression, of habitation, of this very existence.

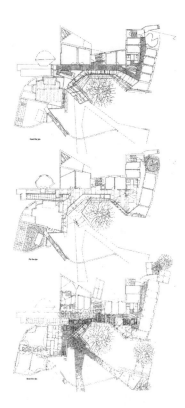

Figure 3.12a Youth Music School, Hamburg (1997–2000). Design: E. Miralles & B. Tagliabue. Maquette.

Source: El Croquis 2005, Enric Miralles + Bendetta Tagliabue 1995–2000, no 100–101: p. 250, maquette; p. 252, floor plans; pp. 263, 259, 265. © Photograph, EL CROQUIS

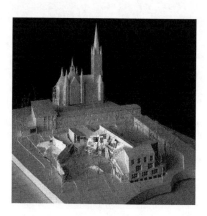

Figure 3.12b Youth Music School, Hamburg (1997–2000). Floor plans.

Source: El Croquis 2005, Enric Miralles + Bendetta Tagliabue 1995–2000, no 100–101: p. 250, maquette; p. 252, floor plans; pp. 263, 259, 265. © Photograph, EL CROQUIS

Figure 3.13 Youth Music School, Hamburg (1997–2000). Interior common space.

Source: El Croquis 2005, Enric Miralles + Bendetta Tagliabue 1995–2000, no 100–101: p. 250, maquette; p. 252, floor plans; pp. 263, 259, 265. © Photograph, EL CROQUIS

Figure 3.14a Youth Music School, Hamburg (1997–2000). Interior common space.

Source: El Croquis 2005, Enric Miralles + Bendetta Tagliabue 1995–2000, no 100–101: p. 250, maquette; p. 252, floor plans; pp. 263, 259, 265. © Photograph, EL CROQUIS

Figure 3.14b Youth Music School, Hamburg (1997–2000). View of the interior common space.

Source: El Croquis 2005, Enric Miralles + Bendetta Tagliabue 1995–2000, no 100–101: p. 250, maquette; p. 252, floor plans; pp. 263, 259, 265. © Photograph, EL CROQUIS

The fluid/liquid spatiality of the school buildings we have talked about is at once bold and restrained. Bold because it frees the public part of the school from any reminder of an institutional character and at the same time pushes it into limit forms and degrees of complexity in favour of a fluid chronotope of social interactions. Restrained because it takes shape within an institutional condition that sets limits on the global school spatio-temporal function. In these terms 'spatiality' resists the exaggerated fluidity we see in other contemporary projects – for example the MVRDV-designed Villa VPRO in Hilversum (an office building with a luxuriously fluid working environment that dissolves any sense of order and pre-designed organisation) at the Danish Pavilion at the Architecture Biennale 2010, in Beijing, designed by Bjarke Ingels, with its ramp rippling all the way up the building, sweeping along with it any concept of 'closed' or 'open', 'inside' or 'outside', 'motion' and 'stillness' – a spatio-temporal fluidity that blurs marks and material boundaries with an elegant impudence.

From our contemporary hyper-modern age we will move back into the past, to the period of the modern movement and specifically to the work of Bidinost (Bidinost, Sakamoto, Guevara et al. 2010; Conenna & Tsoukala 2012), to see how he handled the common public space of the school in a place where the climate dictates a semi-outdoor solution. With inventive virtuosity he designed ways not to lose the sense of sociality that a different content gave the modern architectural spirit. We may say that in the specific educational environment the functional goes beyond its instrumental relation with its users to emerge as a structural element of its social aspect. This coordination of the functional and the social evolves in an open public space (courtyard), which in turn is constituted and given shape by the protective form of the roof. Here we have a reversal of the predominant relation between the full and the empty, spatially and symbolically (Figure 3.15).

This empty public space, a place of social congregation and dealings, agent of a free active behaviour and discourse, gives this school its identity. It is what contains the closed learning cores and not what is contained in a closed system of educational spaces defined by them. This conceptual and symbolic reversal makes the Manuel Belgrano school a paradigm of architecture with a social-pedagogical identity. The functional elements of the programme are placed freely in this empty space like the objects in a Purist painting, and on the building's ground floor. The teaching areas (classroom and laboratory wing), isolated units freely positioned in space, which co-exist in the time of the educational and social activities without tensions and conflicts but also without conventional harmonies, engage and interact beneath the same roof. An expressive horizontal surface whose curved end rises in dynamic elegance towards the sky and whose generous shade

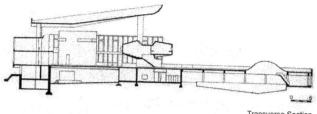

Transverse Section

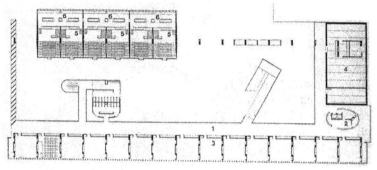

Plan of Level +8.60m

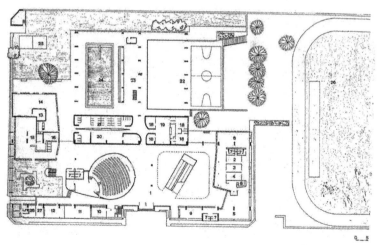

Ground Floor Plan

Figure 3.15 Manuel Belgrano School, Cordoba, Argentina (1960–1971). Design:
O. Bidinost, J. Chute. Floor plans and section.

Source: Bidinost, V., Sakamoto, Á., Guevara, C., García, T., Mele, J. et al. (2010). *Bidinost.*
Buenos Aires: FADU (Facultad de Arquitectura, Diseño y Urbanismo), Universidad de Buenos
Aires: p. 62, Planta baja; p. 63, Planta nivel + 8.60m. © Drawings, Veronicá Bidinost

embraces the several units of the teaching space is the trademark feature of this monument.

The roof, a term of multiple significance like all architectural elements, signifies protection. The form of the roof, the material it is made of and its size and colour all contribute to the perceived image and emotional response to it. How a space is roofed is declarative of the way of life that unfolds within its boundaries. It is also indicative of the climate and the ecological, physical characteristics of the locality of which the building is to be a part. Bidinost's roof utilises the properties of concrete, hearkens to the moods of the natural, biotopical forces and aspires to share in the dynamic of the social life that plays out in the leisure moments of the young people beneath its shelter. Its dynamic, expressionistic form, free and disengaged from the boundaries of the spaces it is designed to protect, creates a semi-outdoor space that can accommodate all the members of the educational community and draw the eyes of all the isolated spatial units (Figures 3.16a–b and 3.17a–b).

Some of these units rise upwards and seem to float in the air; others grow out of the ground itself, forming a hard windbreak to shelter life in the courtyard from chilly breezes. Roof and volumes work together to create

Figure 3.16a Manuel Belgrano School, Cordoba, Argentina (1960–1971). Design: O. Bidinost, J. Chute. Views of the semi-cover space.

Source: Architect Claudio Conenna's archive. © Photograph, Claudio Conenna

Figure 3.16b Manuel Belgrano School, Cordoba, Argentina (1960–1971). Views of the semi-cover space.

Source: Architect Claudio Conenna's archive. © Photograph, Claudio Conenna

Figure 3.17a Manuel Belgrano School, Cordoba, Argentina (1960–1971). View of the building.

Source: Architect Claudio Conenna's archive, Architect Ismael Eyres's archive. © Photograph, Claudio Conenna

Figure 3.17b Manuel Belgrano School, Cordoba, Argentina (1960–1971). View of the semi-cover space.

Source: Architect Claudio Conenna's archive, Architect Ismael Eyres's archive. © Photograph, Ismael Eyres

a pleasant micro-climate, where people can comfortably spend their free time. Pure shapes and colours reminiscent of cubism fit together beneath the expressionistic roof, which confidently appeals to the emotions not only with its form but also with its patent intent to shift the weight from a guided didactic-cognitive function of the educational environment to a free social-productive-cognitive one. If the first function corresponds to the pure cubist logic of the several volumes/areas of the educational organism, the second corresponds to the open semi-outdoor space with its emotional facets as these are shaped within the protective and expressionistic intentionality of the roof. Its appearance and its shade, its shelter and its daring, feed the desire to inhabit the environment of knowledge and social engagement. The empty space it creates surrounds the closed volumes, exposes itself freely to their regard and unhindered by prior formations becomes a backdrop for free communication and action, a space of multiple functions and experiential situations, multiply signified and expressive. It is from this reversal of roles between the empty and the full (in an educational environment) that Bidinost's idiolect springs, bold and generous in its architectural and educational expression. To paraphrase Georges Braque's famous comment, that *'the vase gives shape to emptiness, and music to silence'*, we might say that the empty space in Bidinost's architecture gives meaning to form. The empty space corresponds to the music, and the closed built cells to the silence. The spirit, the intellectuality, the meaning of the work is condensed in the immaterialty of the architecture and the music.

The examples we have cited display gradations of fluid spatiality. In Bidinost's school the semi-outdoor space, sheltered by the poetic art of the roof, is crossed by the sizeable ramp leading to the classroom wing with the balconies projecting into its domain. A spartan void, fluid space flowing towards the open space of the school organised on the roof of the basement sports facilities – empty space serving as a foil to the roof, which encourages congregation without the playful provocativeness of irregular labyrinthine corridors. In the schools of Hertzberger, Behnisch and Miralles, on the other hand, the void is not at rest. It builds up from the vertiginous movement of the ramps, stairs and bridges that cross it, throwing open the world of the Lacanian 'Real', inviting the contingency of the momentary into the daily routine of the school. A dynamic void, complexly structured and irregularly composed, goads one to perpetual intense bodily experience, converting fluidity into flux, but, due to the limitations imposed by the institutional character of its function, without the whole built school environment sharing in this restless atmosphere.

Modality 3: breadth of form, multiplicity, transcending boundaries

The architectural discussion on allusive form and open-ended space began in the middle of the twentieth century, when human psychological and existentialist needs and cultural differences were recognised as design data. This recognition implied a new angle of vision for architecture. The architectural object had to be more flexible, even 'neutral', in its form and structure – 'open' and 'adaptable' to different ways of life, different needs and desires, a dynamic field with fluid semantic boundaries that can be adjusted to accommodate the particularities of those who experience and inhabit them. By the end of the century the question was (and still is) being discussed with greater urgency as it became associated with the 'freedom' and 'singularity' of each individual user of a specific space. From deconstruction to the current post-structuralist trends, the concept of the boundary has been diverted materially and dissolved semantically using such tools as 'blurring', 'hints', 'superimpositions', 'confetti', 'collage', 'montage', 'follies' and 'voids'. All these express the zeal of certain architects to overcome the obstacles of the established architectural idiom and ensure a participative, strongly experiential and interactive condition of the user with the space he inhabits. In this endeavour it is not unreasonable for architects to turn to the concepts of drifting and play (Lucan 2010; Scoffier 2011).

How far can one experiment and apply these conceptual architectural tools in the case of school buildings, which operate within the bounds of an institutional logic? If any architect can claim to have extensive knowledge and practical experience in the matter, it is Herman Hertzberger. In his theoretical and applied work we find a rich store of reflection on the complex educational environment. It is not only the labyrinthine, Piranesian collective space of the schools he designed (we presented examples of his work in earlier chapters) and the single learning landscape, as he called the school complex with its challenging dispersion of stimuli and varied organisation. He also raises and deals with questions like 'breadth of form'. Musing on the interpretability of form, he was led to the concept of adaptability – that is 'the accommodating capacity of form, which allows it to be filled with associations and thus bring about a mutual dependence with the users' (Hertzberger 2002: 150). He was concerned with the breadth of form upon which the interaction of form and user depended, the experience and appropriation of form. This in turn is connected with his own self-criticism and the criticism of other theoreticians and practitioners of architecture on the qualities of predetermined form, the strict and unchallengeable boundaries of its interpretation and use. The preplanned and predetermined are replaced by multiplicity, the capacity for constantly eliciting new and unforeseen uses and interpretations of form. One micro-architectural example of this is the brick podium block he placed in a central position in the hall of the Montessori school in Delft. As he points out, the potential of this space for assemblies and spontaneous gatherings would be greater if this block could be moved out of the way from time to time. But he felt that this very permanence at the heart of this collective space made it a focal point containing incentives for response, broadening the spectrum of its potential and possible uses (Figures 3.18a–b). The platform is used in various ways, is capable of multiple interpretations and can be extended in all directions using modular wooden elements that are stored inside it and can transform it into a stage. The negative of this podium is found in the corresponding space in the school's kindergarten. Here we find a recessed square filled with wooden blocks in the form of low stools. These can easily be removed

Figure 3.18a Montessori School, Delft (1966–70). Brick podium block.

Source: Hertzberger, H. (2008). *Space and Learning: Lessons in Architecture 3*. Rotterdam: nai010: p. 99, f. 5. © Photograph, Johan van de Keuken

Figure 3.18b Montessori School, Delft (1966–70). Brick podium block.

Source: Hertzberger, H. (1991). *Lessons for Students in Architectures.* Rotterdam: nai010: p. 153, f. 399. © Photograph, Herman Hertzberger

and arranged in various ways, both in the hollow and elsewhere, depending on how they are to be used, in free or guided play. Hertzberger wrote of this feature that

> Just as the podium-block evokes images and associations with climbing a hill to get a better view, so the square hollow gives a feeling of seclusion, a retreat, and evokes associations of descending into a valley or a hollow. If the platform block is an island in the sea, the hollow square is a lake, which the children have turned into a swimming pool by adding a diving board.

(Hertzberger 1991: 154)

Part of the outdoor space is organised in the same way. Parallel low walls create areas intended for sand boxes and gardens, but which can also be freely rearranged to accommodate many other uses. The very material used to build these low walls (perforated building blocks) enables them to be put to many different uses. The same way of looking at things is apparent in a secondary school in Villiers-lés-Nancy, France, designed by Remy Butler in 1990. His intention was that the architecture of the school would work towards an atmosphere of de-institutionalisation. The structural volumes are arranged along an axis that functions as an internal 'street'. Its parabolic shape ripples the interior surface, abolishing the distinction of boundaries between floor and walls. The slope of the wall suggests unexpected uses and behaviours, giving this public part of the school a playful character. Similar thinking governs the design of school libraries where walls and bookcases create seating areas, cosy spaces for study or relaxation.

What Hertzberger stresses in his text is his disagreement with the notion that the role of architecture is to devise bare shells, as unemphatic and neutral as possible (Hertzberger 1991). This, in his view, could lead to a sort of paralysis, since an absolutely neutral architecture would elicit no associations. And it is the quality of space to evoke associations, to stir up one's experiences and suggest living conditions for the proposed new spatial context that Hertzberger sees as of primary importance for the inhabitant of the space. And herein lies the difference between his approach and those of contemporary post-structuralist currents in architecture, where the very concept of form is abandoned together with all its baggage, from aesthetics and its set of rules to its semantic mechanisms and programmed behaviour. Modern electronic technology and biotechnology are harnessed as a means and a structural element of the construction of space, material and mental. Fluidity succeeds signs, their permanent or controlled multiplicity, making the body and its desires a factor regulating its place of residence. Neutral forms have yielded to fluid topomorphies that are in no danger of becoming patterns and congealing into new signifiers with their repetitive reproduction, fixed symbols in an historical time. Contingency and imagination constitute the new forms in the processes of creating space.

Recourse to stories is reasonable in the case of the organisation of educational spaces in the context of those approaches. The imaginary world of the story is a source of images that are free of the signs of the real and at the same time are contained within children's experience as an inseparable part of their perceptual relation with the world. This paradox is the basis of the work done by Susanne Hofmann and her students – the Baupiloten – at Berlin's Technical University. Using stories and the interpretive power of the imagination of the children taking part in the processes of conceiving space, the Baupiloten create playful learning landscapes offering play, imagination and the freedom they promise as incentives to knowledge. This playful atmosphere is the essence of the Taka Tuka Land kindergarten, the geometrically irregular volume of its façade unifying the interior and exterior space, offering incentives for all kinds of activities in its enigmatic, enticingly indeterminate (functionally undefined) intermediate spaces. In the case of the Galilei primary school the Baupiloten worked with the children to improve the quality of the traffic areas in the existing building with the aim of transforming straightforward corridors into a dynamic field for informal activity and social life. Another of their projects involved the redesign of the century-old Erika Mann Primary School. Working with the school's pupils to implement the experimental concept that 'Form Follows Children's Fiction', the Baupiloten created a second shell covering the floors and ceilings inside the building in an interpretation of the 'Snuffle of the Silver Dragon'. The folds of the soft material used form interactive 'caves', 'refuges', 'platforms', places to sit, relax, get away or join in social activities.

In other buildings – and especially in nursery schools – form is conceived as a plaything through the re-interpretation of objects that stimulate the children's imagination. Günter Behnisch created such a building using the idea of a ship. Ground plan and façades, through shape, line and surface, with the bold and playful deconstructivist arrangement of the features of the 'ship', create an enticing atmosphere for the children, since they identify their inhabitation of that space with play. Imagination and reality interact to promote the goals of recreational, stimulative, experiential learning.

We will close this unit with the ultra-contemporary project designed by Anna Heringer – namely the METI Handmade School in Rudrapur, Bangladesh (Hertzberger, Heringer, Vassal et al. 2013). The poetics of this fine building relate not to storytelling but to physical structures with a dual character: on the one hand they are symbolically empty, and on the other as part of the child's fantasy world they bridge the gap between the real and the imaginary. Here the empty collective space is given the form of a tunnel (associatively referring to an underground lair or den) passing through the filled space, an unbuilt pocket within the built environment, a desymbolised space within the programmatically constructed space, as proposed in the initial design by Rem Koolhaas (Lucan 2010) – a semantically denatured space that welcomes the voluntary free activity of the children, the instantaneous time of their desires (Figures 3.19a–b and 3.20a–b). Anna Heringer, like her mentor Herman Hertzberger, uses basic architectural/ structural elements to give space a playful polyphonic character. She handles the syntax of architecture with exceptional skill, evolving new equilibria without, as we have said, having recourse to mythical representations. Using the cheapest materials and the most rudimentary technology, and harnessing a wide-ranging contributory participation, she has succeeded in organising an environment that is simple and at the same time rich, eco-friendly, educationally stimulating and architecturally innovative (Hertzberger, Heringer, Vassal et al. 2013).

Figure 3.19a METI School, Rudrapur, Bangladesh (2005–2006). Design: A. Heringer. View of the building.

Source: Kurt Hoerbst's archive, STUDIO Anna Heringer's archive. © Photograph, Kurt Hoerbst

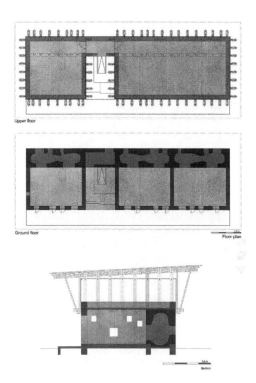

Figure 3.19b METI School, Rudrapur, Bangladesh (2005–2006). Floor plans and section.

Source: Kurt Hoerbst's archive, STUDIO Anna Heringer's archive. © Drawings, Anna Heringer

Figure 3.20a METI School, Rudrapur, Bangladesh (2005–2006). Interior learning space.

Source: Kurt Hoerbst's archive. © Photograph, Kurt Hoerbst

Figure 3.20b METI School, Rudrapur, Bangladesh (2005–2006). Interior common
        space.

Source: Kurt Hoerbst's archive. © Photograph, Kurt Hoerbst

Notes

1 We know that since the Renaissance man has privileged vision, the sense that
   more than any other is associated with reason, perception and control. It was not
   until the twentieth century that its role was challenged and the contribution of the
   other senses to the Subject's relation with his surroundings acknowledged. This
   investigation is condensed in the term 'bodily experience' initially in the context
   of phenomenological views of the perception, understanding and interpretation of
   the environment and later in that of the post-structuralist approaches that invest
   in graphic bodily action – gesture, expression, perambulation. The distinction
   between body/senses and mind ceases to exist and the Subject (submission to the
   rule or foundation of the ego in the reason and will of the individual) is renamed a
   singularity (the 'I' as integral combination of the inner powers of the individual).
   Like other arts, architecture responds to these contemporary considerations with
   the interactive fluid built environments it proposes.

2 One great advantage of the green roof is the improvement of the microclimate,
   since plants lower the air temperature, absorb carbon dioxide and release precious
   oxygen, in short supply in an urban environment. Through the reflective ability
   of their leaves, and their absorption of much of the sun's radiation for their biological functions (photosynthesis, respiration), plants protect the roof from the
   thermal loads of the sun's radiation and lower the temperature locally by 3° to
   7° C. The foliage on green roofs also helps filter particles from the air, reducing

the amount deposited on stone, metal or concrete surfaces. Also, the rainwater that would otherwise end up in the drainage system serves to water the plants, reducing runoff by up to 90 per cent, while at the same time the water retained by the grass and flowers gradually evaporates, cooling the surrounding area. The roof also serves as a laboratory environment where the children can study these environmental qualities. Nor is the educational quality of a green roof on a school confined to science lessons, since the potential of such a space (ecosystem) makes it an experiential environment, where the children interact with and learn from nature. Optical, aural, olfactory and tactile stimuli increase the degree of complexity of the environment, sharpening their perceptions and cognitive processes (see Pouniou, Despoina 2014, *Environmental Education and School Architecture*. Diploma Research Thesis, Supervisor: K. Tsoukala).

A few final words

Fluid space and transformational learning

We have reflected on the qualities of a built school environment that shifts the focus from child-centred to relational-centred education, aiming at an educational framework that is morally committed, democratic and participative in its operation, cooperative, articulating the intrapsychic with the interpsychic through emotional experience. We have pondered the experiential relation between child and place that contributes to the cultivation of a sense of responsibility for his lived environment and the development of his cognitive processes (where the school space is itself a source of information about the material world, technology and culture).

Drawing on experiment, theory and philosophy, we devised three spatial qualities, three conceptual munitions that mediate the relation between new pedagogical approaches and the architecture of the educational environment – three passage concepts bringing us to the chronotopes of contemporary educational practice. Let us not look in these terms for the defined causal links of scientific discourse or Weberian interpretation through ideal types. Those cases use a conceptual toolkit in the framework of a linear, progressive succession of logical steps. The three concepts we propose appropriate internal boundaries in favour of an open-ended, transformative, potential process that is not designed on the basis of a deterministic linear logic. Hence, while Weber's ideal types are characterised by abstractions and constitute a kind of model, and the scientific conceptual toolkit is universalised, tending to establish fixed ideotypes independent of the times, conditions or situations, in our approach the conceptualisations concern shifts and transformations to conditions of uncertain equilibrium and intensification. When Bakhtin speaks of polyphony, he is not proposing an analytical tool for understanding and interpreting a phenomenon, but is identifying the suspended passage of the interior boundary, the meeting of self and otherness, with the dynamic potential for an expansion of limits and the emergence of something new. In this condition of transindividuality, of relational ontology, mental individuation and social individuation are not understood as two separate, polarised, ambi-articulated individuations consonant with a dyadic development model. In an transindividual situation something internal and something external take place at the same time, a simultaneous dual individuation, mental and collective. The concepts of polyphonic and playful space that we propose are inscribed in this perspective of relational ontology, and the concept of activated space, particularly in an educational context, intensifies the building of the moral bond, the commitment of responsibility to the other as described by Vygotsky (see the zone of proximal development as discussed in Chapter 1) or today by educator Tony Shallcross. As has been said in earlier chapters, activated space does not respond intelligently or combinatively but in the end mechanically to the action of the child, but as a cultural-material field engages in his activities through the perspective of his responsible commitment to the collectivity. Herein lies the difference between activated space and the quality of responsiveness defined by Piaget, who makes the dynamic and the role of praxis dependent on the child's mental processes with the capacity of the material environment to act transformatively on his activities. This is a responsiveness, an addressivity, of the material non-mediated by the historical-cultural condition within which it operates. Finally, the three concepts proposed – activated, polyphonic and playful space – bring to the fore the role of bodily experience in the making of space-time without circumscribing this experience within a phenomenological point of view, a dimension of individual corporeal space. The three proposed qualities relate to transindividuality and the plural body of social collective space, escaping the identifying and rhizomatic phenomenological approaches favouring an intensive and potential metastable 'order', in favour of an uncertain equilibrium of activated potentialities and diversions of spatial-temporal sequences and inevitable deterministic hierarchies.

These spatial qualities constitute a multimodal source of significant corporeal practices offering the child the possibility of comparison by constantly transforming his habitual semantically charged spatio-social experience. Some educationists think that in childhood physical expressivity is not boxed up in bipolar forms of effective reflective action but wanders and fluctuates with a disposition to adventure and discovery. Consequently, in the school setting the learning and psychopedagogic process should preferably liberate and not curb these roaming activities and should not be confined to proven methods. The spatial qualities proposed heighten the discontinuity and the unpredictability of these physical expressions, reinforcing the imagined narrative space of the dialogical communicational act. The degree of dialogicality of the material spatial framework is thus folded into the degrees of polysemy, of bodily freedom of expression and unimpeded-surprise human interaction. The interface of a communicational-collaborative-experiential pedagogy with a polyphonic material spatial field escalates the significant trying-out choices of the children and the possibilities of the spatial-temporal vagaries of the environment in the child's unrestricted impromptu activity in the framework of a commitment of responsibility towards others. Through this dialogical relationship with the other and with the spatial material context the child tests and reconstructs the social frameworks/points he inhabits. Building constantly on the fluid boundary between himself and the other, the child appropriates the world around him, inscribing and interweaving his voice into the multiplicity, going beyond mere compliance with specific educational practices.

What we propose, then, beyond the diffusion of educational activities throughout the totality of a school space rich in diverse stimuli, is the capacity of that space to change, to be transformed, to engage polyphonically with the environment and its users, to be interactive, dynamic, fluid, and playful, with a constant flow of challenging and renewing derogations from established spatial-social codes. These modalities, together with fluent, fluid spatiality, irregularly labyrinthine space, and the turbulent movement of the void, invoke the individual-within-the-universal and constitute preconditions for alertness and creative digressions.

The synergy and involvement of those spatial qualities contribute to the creation of educational spaces in the spirit of transformative, collaborational, experiential learning. By contrast, over-stressing any of them in isolation removes structural elements from the dual plane of spatial construction and educational context. Also, the creation of space or its reduction to a kind of playful construct depends on how the architectural elements and techniques are handled. This difference is illustrated by the comparison of examples cited in our consideration of the modalities of space. The school environments of Hertzberger, Behnisch, Miralles and Heringer orchestrate diverse contrasting elements with extraordinary skill in a moving poetic synthesis that engages the individual in a rich experiential spatial-social educational experience. On the other hand, architects who resort to myths reproducing imagined spatial forms may superficially submit with the formal and symbolic mythopoetic nature of their proposals, but in the end they reduce space to a playful construct, a kind of play-area, where the mythical predominates, is established as the exclusive tool for handling the spatial-educational qualities, with the concomitant loss of 'architectural idiom' (and here we mean not the language of rigid grammar and inflexible syntax but the language of continuous transformative process).

From Disneyland to the Parc de la Villette – both of them amusement parks – there is an unbridgeable conceptional and cultural difference. In the case of Disneyland imagination and desire are freed through the replacement of the hard, symbolic social framework by another, equally predetermined and pre-designed, framework of mythical representations. At the Parc de la Villette the release of those forces is triggered by the banishment of symbols, paradoxical correlations, unexpected co-ordinations, the invitation to wandering, the ironic and collisional handling of opposites. The release of the human creative forces (of imagination and desire) is a complex process, requiring a poetics of the space of coordinated and transformative bodily experience that can guarantee a synergy of technical skill, imagination and reflection – all within a condition of participative processes that result in awareness, stimulation, excitement and not the logic of repetitions that, however fruitful, are limited to the automatisms of a planned methodical cyclicity.

Bibliography

Badiou, Alain (2008). *Peut-on penser la politique?* Translated by Dimitris Verge-tis & Tasos Bentzelos. Addendum: Dimitris Vergetis. Athens: Pataki (In Greek).

Bakhtin, Mikhail (2000). *Problems of Dostoevsky's Poetics* (1929). Translated by Alexandra Ioannidou. Edited by Vaggelis Chatzivasiliou. Athens: Polis (In Greek).

Bakirtzis, Konstantinos N. (1996). *The Dynamic of Interaction in Communication: Critical Presentation of Kurt Lewin, Jacob Moreno and Carl Rogers' Contributions.* Athens: Gutenberg (In Greek).

Bakirtzis, Konstantinos N. (2004). *Communication and Education.* Athens: Gutenberg (In Greek).

Bauman, Zygmunt (2007). *Liquid Love: On the Frailty of Human Bonds.* Translated by Giorgos Karabelas. Athens: Metechmio (In Greek).

Bauman, Zygmunt (2008). *Liquid Times: Living in an Age of Uncertainty.* Translated by Konstantinos D. Geormas. Athens: Metechmio (In Greek).

Bennett, Neville, Andreae, Jenny, Hegarty, Philip & Wade, Barbara (1980). *Open Plan Schools: Schools Council Project.* London: NFER.

Bidinost, Verónica, Sakamoto, Ángel, Guevara, Celia, García, Tomás, Mele, Jorge et al. (2010). *Bidinost.* Buenos Aires: FADU (Facultad de Arquitectura, Diseño y Urbanismo), Universidad de Buenos Aires.

Blundell Jones, Peter (2000). *Günter Behnisch.* Basel: Studio Paperback.

Boesiger, Willy (ed.) (1964). *Richard Neutra 1923–50: Buildings and Projects.* Introduction: Sigfried Giedion. Zurich: Verlag fur Architektur.

Bosch, Rosan (2013). "Designing for a Better World Starts at School: Rosan Bosch at TEDxIndianapolis." http://www.youtube.com/watch?v=q5mpeEa_VZo (last access 17–11–2013).

Clot, Yves (ed.) (1999). *Avec Vygotsky.* Paris: La Dispute.

Conenna, Claudio & Tsoukala, Kyriaki (2012). "Architecture and Collective Qualities of Public Space: The Case of Manuel Belgrano School, Architects: O. Bidinost, J. Chute & Collaborators." In: *youth.www.public space. Undisciplined Gatherings + Oblique Passages*, edited by Kyriaki Tsoukala, Lila Pantelidou et al., 167–184. Thessaloniki: Epikentro (In Greek).

Doise, Willem & Mugny, Gabriel (1981). *Le développement social de l'intelligence.* Paris: InterEditions.

Emerson, Caryl (December 1983). "The Outer Word and Inner Speech: Bakhtin, Vygotsky and the Internalization of Language." *Critical Inquiry*, 10 (2), 245–264.

Fragos, Christos (1983). *Positions on Education*. Athens: Gutenberg (In Greek).

Germanos, Dimitris (2004). *Space and Educational Process: The Pedagogical Quality of Space*. Athens: Gutenberg (In Greek).

Hertzberger, Herman (1991). *Lessons for Students in Architecture*. Rotterdam: nai010.

Hertzberger, Herman (2000). *Space and the Architect: Lessons in Architecture 2*. Rotterdam: nai010.

Hertzberger, Herman (2008). *Space and Learning: Lessons in Architecture 3*. Rotterdam: nai010.

Hertzberger, Herman, Heringer, Anna, Vassal, Jean Philip et al. (2013). *The Future of Architecture*. Rotterdam: nai010.

Huizinga, Johan (2010). *Homo Ludens*. Translated by Gerasimos Lykiardopoulos & Stephanos Rosanis. Edited by Panagiotis Kondylis. Athens: Gnosi (In Greek).

Kalafati, Eleni & Papalexopoulos, Dimitris (2006). *Takis X. Zenetos: Virtual Visions and Architecture*. Athens: Libro.

Krier, Leon (1998). *Architecture Choice or Fate*. Great Britain: Andreas Papadakis.

Lefaivre, Liane & Döll ab (2007). *Ground-Up City: Play as a Design Tool*. Rotterdam: nai010.

Lewin, Kurt (1959). *Psychologie dynamique*. Paris: PUF.

Lipovats, Thanos & Romanos, Vasilis (2002). *The Subject in Post-Modernity*. Athens: Nisos (In Greek).

Lucan, Jacques (2010). *Composition, non-composition: Architecture et théories, XIXe–XXe siècles*. Lausanne: Presses Polytechniques et Universitaires Romandes.

Miralles, Enric (2005). "Escuela de Musica de Hamburgo." *Enric Miralles + Bendetta Tagliabue 1995–2000, El Croquis*, nos. 100–101, 238–267.

Moore, Gary T. (1987). "The Physical Environment and Cognitive Development in Child Care Centers." In: *Spaces for Children: The Built Environment and Child Development*, edited by Carol S. Weinstein & Thomas G. David. New York: Plenum Press, 41–72.

Newman, Fred & Holzman, Lois (1996). *Unscientific Psychology: A Cultural-Performatory Approach to Understanding Human Life*. London: Praeger.

Ouggrinis, Konstantinos-Alketas (2012). *Transformable Architecture: Motion, Adaptation, Flexibility*. Athens: Omilos Ion (In Greek).

Pesic, Jelena M. & Baucal, Aleksandar (January–February 1996). "Vygotsky and Psychoanalysis." *Journal of Russian and East European Psychology*, 34 (1), 33–39.

Piaget, Jean & Inhelder, Bärbel (1947). *La représentation de l'espace chez l'enfant*. Paris: PUF.

Quentin, Stevens (2007). *The Ludic City: Exploring the Potential of Public Spaces*. London and New York: Routledge.

Reginald, Isaacs (1983). *Gropius: An Illustrated Biography of the Creator of the Bauhaus*. Boston, Toronto and London: Bulfinch Press Book.

Renaut, Alain (2009). *La Philosophie*. Translated by Tasos Bentzelos. Edited by Aris Stylianou. Athens: Polis (In Greek).

Rossi, Aldo (1981). *L'architecture de la ville*. Paris: L'Equerre.

Sadler, Simon (1998). *The Situationist City*. Cambridge: The MIT Press.

Scoffier, Richard (2011). *Les quatre concepts fondamentaux de l'architecture contemporaine*. Paris: NORMA.

Shallcross, Tony, Robinson, John, Pace, Paul, Wals, Arjen & Bezzina, Christopher (2009). *Creating Sustainable Environments in Our Schools*. Edited by Konstantia Tamoutseli. Thessaloniki: Epikentro (In Greek).

Terragni, Attilio, Libeskid, Daniel & Rosselli Paolo (2004). *The Terragni Atlas: Built Architecture*. Milan: SKIRA.

Todorov, Tzvetan (1994). *Critique de la critique, un roman d'apprentissage*. Translated by Giannis Kiourtsakis. Edited by Trisevgeni Papaioannou. Athens: Polis (In Greek).

Tsoukala, Kyriaki (2000). *Trends in School Design: From Child-Centred Functionalism to the Post-Modern Approach*. 2nd edition, supplemented, revised. Thessaloniki: Paratiritis (In Greek).

Tsoukala, Kyriaki (2001). *L'Image de la ville chez l'enfant*. Paris: Anthropos.

Tsoukala, Kyriaki (2006). *Children's Urban Locality: Architecture and Mental Representations of Space*. Athens: Typothito Editions (In Greek).

Tsoukala, Kyriaki (2007). *Les territoires urbaines de l'enfant*. Paris: L'Harmattan.

Tsoukala, Kyriaki (2009). "Spatial Representation, Activity, and Meaning: Children's Images of the Contemporary City." In *SEMIOTICA, Spatial Meaning*, volume 2009, issue 175, 77–135.

Tsoukala, Kyriaki & Voyatzaki, Maria (2004). "The school space as a means of environmental conscience construction: The contribution of architecture and landscape construction methods and materials to the pedagogic quality of space." In *Proceedings of the 14th annual Conference of the European Early Childhood research Association: Quality in Early Childhood Education*. Malta: University of Malta.

Ulmann, Jacques (1982). *La pensée éducative contemporaine*. Paris: Vrin.

van den Heuvel, Willem-Jan (1992). *Structuralism in Dutch Architecture*. Rotterdam: nai010.

Vygotsky, Lev S. (1993). *Thought and Language* (1934). Athens: Gnosi (In Greek).

Vygotsky, Lev S. (1997). *Mind in Society* (1934). Translated by Anna Bibou & Stella Vosniadou. Edited by Stella Vosniadou. Athens: Gutenberg (In Greek).

Wertsch, James V. (1985). *Vygotsky and the Social Formation of Mind*. Cambridge, Massachusetts and London, England: Harvard University Press.

Zizek, Slavoj (2009). *How to Read Lacan*. Translated by Dimitris Kalagiaris & Konstantinos Papadakis. Edited by Dimitris Vergetis & Alexia Paraskevoulakou. Athens: Pataki (In Greek).

Index

absence/void xvii, xix, 2, 5, 8, 17, 22, 33, 64
activated space xiv, xv, xvi, xvii, xviii, 3, 13–16, 20, 63
activity 2; intersubjective xvii
adaptability 26, 54
affective-emotional experience xv
Aghios Dimitrios school (Athens) 26–7
Albert Schweizer Special School (Bad Rappenau) 40, 43
alienation xvii, 6, 8, 17
Amersham School 26
anthropology: cultural 19; of space 18
anti-psychology 8
Antonio Sant'Elia nursery school 23
Apollo schools (Amsterdam) 35–7
appropriation 14, 21, 29, 54
Aragon, Louis 19
Archi5 30
Archigram 18
architecture: Baroque 34, 44; contemporary 19, 34; digital-potential 18; of educational spaces 4, 12–20; endless 18; and interdisciplinarity xiii; inter-war 23; and pedagogy 20–1n1; post-structuralist 16, 19, 26, 28, 33, 40, 53; and psychology xi; and social practices xii; theory and criticism of xi
architectural promenade 18
architectural space xiii, xvii
Architecture Biennale 48
Architecture of the City, The (Rossi) 12–13
Archizoom 18
automatic writing 19

Badiou, Alain 17
Bakhtin, Mikhail xvii, 2, 7, 8, 16–17, 62
Bakirtzis, Konstantinos N. 10
Barcelona Pavilion 22
Bauman, Zygmunt 28
Baupiloten group 30, 57
Beaudouin, Eugène 23–4
behavioural space xviii
Behnisch, Günter xvii, 13, 34, 40–3, 57, 64
Bennett, Andrew 17
Berlin Technical University 57
Bidinost, O. 34, 48–52, 53
BIGArchitects 30
Binet, Alfred 4
biotechnology 56
blurring 20, 54
bodily experience 60n1
bodily space xix
Bosch, Rosan 31–2
boundaries, transcending i, 3, 20, 53–60
Box house 23
Braque, Georges 53
breadth of form 3, 20, 53–60
Breton, André 19
Bruner, Jerome 4
built environments 4, 58, 60n1
Butler, Remy 56

Cadavre Exquis 23
capitalism xi
Carlo, Giancarlo de 18
child-centredness xiii, 4, 5, 15, 21, 62
child development 28

children: active engagement of 10; as active members of school community 4; relationship with space 14–15
child-scale xiv
chronotope 48, 62
Chute, J. 48–51
classrooms: as closed spatial model xiv; concept of 2; as dwelling-space 14, 23; as learning fields/landscapes 2; learning outside of 12, 13; organisation of 3, 26, 30, 34, 38, 48, 53
collaboration xvii, 2, 7, 9–10, 32, 64
collage 20, 54
collectivism 9
communication 5, 10; plane of 9; role of 5
Communication and Education (Bakirtzis) 10
Constant (Anton Nieuwenhuys) 18
co-operativeness 8
Corona School (Los Angeles) 23, 25
corporeity 14–16
cubism 52
cultural anthropology 19
cultural criticism xv
cultural systems 2
cultural theory xv

Dalton Plan/Projects 9
Danish Pavilion 48
Davis, Richard Llewelyn 18
deconstruction, 28, 53
deconstructivism 33, 40
Decroly, Ovide 26
de-institutionalisation 56
democracy xvii
design: fluid 18; open-ended 18; participatory 18; scientification of xiii
desymbolisation 19
determinism 7
Dewey, John 9
dialogicality 2, 63; differential xvii
dialogical-polyphonic space xv, xvi, xvii, 3, 13, 16–19, 38
dialogical space xvii, 20
dialogical theory 16
differentiated instruction 26
Disneyland 64–5
Dostoevsky, Fyodor 16, 33

drifting 19, 20, 54
dualism 5, 7, 9
Dubuffet, Jean 19
Duhamel, Marcel 19
Duiker, Jan 23
dynamic interaction 10

education: child-centred 9, 15, 62; environmental (EE) 8–9, 30; new xiv, 4; relational-centred 9–10, 62; science of 4–5; teacher-centred xiv, 9
educational modality, architecture of 12–20
educational science 12
educational spaces: built xvii; de-institutionalisation of 13–14; *see also* school buildings
educational theory 4, 9, 30
education for sustainable development (ESD) 8–9
Eiermann, Egon 40
empty space 16, 33, 58
energy flow 10
engagement, active 10
environmental education (EE) 8–9, 30
environment(s): built 4, 58, 60n1; role of 10
epistemology xiii, xv, 2
Erika Mann Primary School 57
Erskine, Ralph 18, 23
Escuela Manuel Belgrano (Argentina) 34, 48–52
event(s) 13, 15, 17, 19, 20, 29, 33, 44
expressionism 14
external/internal speech 5, 6, 15

fetishism and fetishisation xvii, 7, 17, 18
field theory xvii, 5
Finmere School (Oxfordshire) 26
flâneur 19
flexibility 3, 20, 22–32
fluidity 20, 22, 26, 28, 56; spatio-temporal 48; taut 3, 32–53
fluid space/spatiality xiv, 3, 16, 20, 53; and transformational learning 62–5
form, allusive 53
Fragos, Christos 9
freedom 19–20, 57; vs. interactivity 2; of movement 12
Freinet, Celestin 9–10, 15

Freinet elementary schools 10, 15
Freud, Sigmund 16
Freudian theory 7–8
Fry, M, 23, 25
functionalism, child-centred xiii

Galilei primary school 57
geometry, social xiii
globalisation xi, xiv, 1–2, 28
green roof 60–1n2
Gropius, W. 23, 25
group dynamics 9
group work xiv

Häring, Hugo 40
Hart, Roger 18
Heidegger, Martin 33
Heringer, Anna 57–60, 64
Hertzberger, Herman xvii, 2, 12–13,
    34–5, 38–9, 56, 58, 64
heteroglossia 2
Himmelblau, Coop 19
historicity and historicism xvii, 1
Hofmann, Susanne 57
holistic school development 8
homo ludens 13
human bonds 28
Husserl, Edmund xviii
hyperlinguistics 8
hyper-modernity xi, xv, xix, 1, 48

ideal type xvi, xvii, 62
identity 28; change of 33
imagination 14, 18–19, 44, 57, 64–5
Impington Village School 23, 25
individualism 9
individuation: mental 62; social 63
Ingels, Bjarke 48
intelligence, practical 29
interactivity 2–3, 20, 22–32
interdisciplinarity xiii, xiv, xvi
interhuman 8
interior space 3, 26, 31, 32
intermediate-transitional space xiv
internal speech 5, 6, 15
interpsychic 5, 9, 62
interrelationalism 8–9
intersubjectivity xvii
intrapsychic 5, 9, 62
involvement 10

isomorphism xiv, xv; of spatial
    organisation xiv

Jardin d'Email 23
Jones, Peter Blundell 40

Kahn, Louis xii
Koffka, Kurt xviii
Köhler, Wolfgang xviii
Kontaratos, Savvas xix
Koolhaas, Rem 58
Krier, Leon 13
Kristeva, Julia 17

Lacan, Jacques xvii, 2, 8, 16–17, 33
language 5–8; egocentric 14
learning: active 2; communicative/
    dialogical 2; cooperative 2;
    experiential 2; fields of 1; and the
    role of life experience 9; spatial
    diffusion of 12; stimulative 4–11;
    transformational 62–5
learning environments 3
learning field 2
learning landscapes 2–3
learning-play-experience 29
Lebenswelt xviii
Lewin, Kurt xvii, xviii, 5, 9
life experience 9–10
life-space (*espace vital*) xviii
linguistics, structural 8; *see also*
    language
liquidity 28
Liquid Love (Bauman) 28
Liquid Times (Bauman) 28
locality 28
Lods, Jean 17
Lods, Marcel 23–4
Lowe Eveline Primary School
    (Southwark) 26
lunch clubs 32

Manuel Belgrano school (Argentina)
    34, 48–52
Marx, Karl 7
Marxism 6, 8–10
mass production, industrial xiii
materiality xvii
METI Handmade School (Bangladesh)
    57–60

microclimates 30, 52
Mies van der Rohe 22, 40
*Mind in Society: The Development of
    Higher Psychological Processes*
    (Vygotsky) 6
Miralles, Enric xii, xvii, 13, 34, 40,
    44–7, 64
modalities: breadth of form 53–60;
    flexibility 22–32; interactivity
    22–32; multiplicity 53–60; spatial
    continuity 32–53; taut fluidity
    32–53; transcending boundaries
    53–60; transformability 22–32
modernism xiv
modernity xix
Moles, A. Abraham xviii
Montessori, Maria 26
Montessori College Oost (Amsterdam)
    35–6, 38–9
Montessori school (Delft) 54–6
Moore, Gary 14, 18, 29
multiculturalism xvii
multiplicity 20, 53–60
MVRDV 48

Nadja 23
neo-Kantianism xviii
Neutra, Richard 23, 25
new education xiv, 4
non-guidance 5

ontology, relational 62
Oost school (Amsterdam) 35–6,
    38–9
open-air schools 23
open-ended design 18, 36
open-plan schools 3, 26, 32
open teaching movement 3
Other/otherness xvii, 2, 8
Oungrinis, Kostis 32

Parc de la Villette 64–5
Parker, Francis 9
Parkhurst, Helen 9
participatory design 18
participatory software 18
passive activity 2; spatial 10
Paul Chevalier complex (Rillieux-la-
    Pape) 30–1
Paysan de Paris 23

pedagogy 4; and architecture 20–1n1;
    communicational-collaborative-
    experiential 64; contemporary 5
Peponis, John xix
perception 16
perceptual space, psychology of xii
phenomenology xviii, xix, 28, 33, 63
philosophy xv, 15; of repression
Piaget, Jean xviii, 4, 14–16, 28–9, 63
Piranesi, Giovanni Battista 33–5, 38, 54
playful space xv, xvi, xvii, 3, 13, 16,
    19–20, 58, 63–4
politics xv
polyphony 2, 44, 58, 62–4
polysemy 63
post-modernism xiv, 1; social approach
    of xiii
post-structuralism 16, 19, 26, 28, 33,
    40, 53
practical intelligence 29
Prévert, Jacques 19
Price, Cedric 18
pseudo-activities xvii, 6–7, 17
psychoanalysis 9, 19
psychological tools 2, 5–6, 30
psychology 19; and architecture xi;
    developmental 4; environmental 29;
    gestalt xvii; of perceptual space xii;
    of space 29
psychopedagogy 4
psychosociology, of space 18

Rapoport, Amos 18
rationalism 40
relational-centred education 9–10, 62
responsiveness 28–9, 63
Restless Ball 23
Rietveld, Gerrit 22
Rogers, Karl 9
Rohe, Mies van der 22, 40
Rohmer, Élisabeth xviii
roofing 23, 30, 40, 48, 50, 52–3, 60–1n2;
    Montessori school (Delft) 26
roofing materials 30
rootedness 28
Rossi, Aldo 12

safe havens 14
St Benno Grammar School (Dresden)
    40–2

St Quentin-en-Yvelines 13
Sanoff, Henry 18
Scharoun, Hans 14, 40
school architecture *see* educational
    spaces; school buildings
school buildings: in Aghios Dimitrios
    (Greece) 26–7; Albert Schweizer
    Special School (Bad Rappenau) 40,
    43; Amersham School 26; *Antonio
    Sant'Elia nursery school* 23;
    Apollo schools (Amsterdam) 35–7;
    Corona School (Los Angeles) 23,
    25; and education 1; Erika Mann
    Primary School 57; Escuela Manuel
    Belgrano (Argentina) 34, 48–52;
    in Fagnano Olona 13; Finmere
    School (Oxfordshire) 26; flexible
    space in 23; Galilei primary school
    57; Impington Village School
    23, 25; Lowe Eveline Primary
    School (Southwark) 26; Manuel
    Belgrano school (Argentina) 34,
    48–52; METI Handmade School
    (Bangladesh) 57–60; Montessori
    school (Delft) 54–6; Oost school
    (Amsterdam) 35–6, 38–9; open-air
    23; open construction 3, 26, 32; Paul
    Chevalier complex (Rillieux-la-Pape)
    30–1; St Benno Grammar School
    (Dresden) 40–2; at St Quentin-en-
    Yvelines 13; Sembat High School
    (France) 30; semi-outdoor 48,
    53; in Suresnes 23–4; Taka Tuka
    Land kindergarten 57; Technical
    University of Berlin 57; Technical
    University of Crete 32; as tool for
    learning 30; University of Berlin
    30; Vilhelmsro Primary School
    (Denmark) 30; in Villiers-lés-Nancy
    56; Vittra International schools 31;
    Youth Music School (Hamburg) 40,
    44–7; *see also* educational spaces
school development, holistic 8
school environments xiv–xv, 12, 18;
    see also school buildings
school libraries 56
Schröder house 22
self-activity xiv
self-concentration 10
self-management 9

self-regulation 8
Sembat High School (France) 30
Shallcross, Tony 8, 63
sitting islands 32
situationists xvii, 18
situations xvii, 10, 18–20, 35, 38, 40,
    44, 52, 62, 63
Smithson, Alison 18
Smithson, Peter 18
social geometry xiii
socialism 7
sociology 19
space: activated xiv, xv, xvi, xvii, xviii,
    3, 13–16, 20, 63; anthropology
    of 18; architectural xiii, xvii, 29;
    behavioural xviii; bodily xix;
    complex xiv; conceptual dimensions
    of xiv, xviii–xix; construction of
    meaning of xviii; contemporary
    xiv; convertible xiv; and cultural
    production 12; as demarcated void
    22; dialogical xvii, 20; dialogical-
    polyphonic xv, xvi, xvii, 3, 13,
    16–19, 38; educational xvii, 13–14;
    emotional experience of 10; empty
    16, 33, 58; flexible xiv, xvi, 14, 22–3,
    26; fluid xiv, xix, 16, 22, 26, 62–5;
    without hierarchies 20; intermediate-
    transitional xiv; intersubjective 13;
    modalities of xv; notational and
    mental xviii; playful xiv, xv, xvi,
    xvii, 3, 13, 16, 19–20, 58, 63–4;
    production of xiii; psychology of
    xi, xii, 29; psychosociology of 18;
    public xiv, xvii; qualities of xiv, xvii;
    school 10; social dimension of xii,
    xvi; urban xvii, 12–13, 19; variable
    xvi, 1; *see also* spatiality
Space and Learning (Herzberger) 34
spatial activity: passive 10; strategic 10
Spatial Choreographies (Peponis) xix
spatial continuity 32–53
spatiality xix, 22, 32, 34, 38, 40; fluid/
    liquid 3, 20, 48, 53; open-air 34;
    polytonic 44; *see also* space
spatial perception, social element of 15
stimulative learning xv, 4–11
strategic spatial activity 10
structuralism 1
superimposition 54

Super Studio 18
surrealism 19
symbolisation 7, 13
synergy 64

Taka Tuka Land kindergarten 57
Tanguy, Yves 19
taut fluidity 3, 32–53
teacher: dyadic relation of child with 4;
    non-guidance by 5
teaching/education: and school
    architecture 1; theories and practices
    of learning 2
teaching spaces *see* educational spaces;
    school buildings
Technical University of Berlin 57
Technical University of Crete 32
technology: digital 29; electronic 26, 56
Tectoniques 30
Terragni, Giuseppe 23
thought, plateaus of xii, xiv
Todorov, Tzvetan 17
topomorphies 57
transcending boundaries i, 3, 20, 53–60
transformability 22–32
transformational learning 62–5
transindividuality 62–3
*Trends in School Architecture: From
    Child-Centred Functionality to the Post-
    Modern Approach* (Tsoukala) 2, 23

*Trends in School Design: From Child-
    Centred Functionalism to the Post-
    Modern Approach* (Tsoukala) xi, xii,
    xiii, xiv, xv,

unity of theory and practice xiv
University of Berlin 30
urban artefacts 12
utility xvii
utopianism xvi, 18, 33

variability xvi, 1, 3, 14, 20, 26, 28, 30–2
Vilhelmsro Primary School (Denmark) 30
Villa VPRO (Hilversum) 48
Villiers-lés-Nancy school 56
Vittra International schools 31
void xvii, xix, 2, 5, 8, 17, 22, 33, 64
Vygotsky, Lev xvii, 2, 5–8, 14–17,
    20–1n1, 30, 63

Weber, Max xvi
Wittgenstein, Ludwig 6, 18
Woods, Shadrach 18
Word 8

Youth Music School (Hamburg) 40, 44–7

Zenetos, Takis 26–27
zones of proximal development (ZPDs)
    xvii, 2, 5, 7, 14

For Product Safety Concerns and Information please contact our EU representative GPSR@taylorandfrancis.com Taylor & Francis Verlag GmbH, Kaufingerstraße 24, 80331 München, Germany

Printed and bound by CPI Group (UK) Ltd, Croydon, CR0 4YY
11/04/2025
01844009-0010